Euthanasia, Suicide, and Despair:
Can the Bible Help?

Euthanasia, Suicide, and Despair: Can the Bible Help?

Guidance when Faced with Ethical Dilemmas

Michael J. Lowis

Foreword by
Albert Jewell

WIPF & STOCK · Eugene, Oregon

EUTHANASIA, SUICIDE, AND DESPAIR: CAN THE BIBLE HELP?
Guidance when faced with ethical dilemmas

Wipf & Stock
An Imprint of Wipf and Stock Publishers
199 W. 8th Ave., Suite 3
Eugene, OR 97401

www.wipfandstock.com

ISBN 13: 978-1-4982-3294-4

Manufactured in the U.S.A.   10/20/2015

CONTENTS

TABLES

FOREWORD

DR MICHAEL LOWIS HAS an impressively wide-ranging mind. After many years of experience as a microbiologist and a chartered psychologist involved in much academic research, he has latterly taken a degree in theology and already published a book examining Jesus' miracles as recorded in the four Gospels. It has been my privilege to have worked with him on some of his studies into the spirituality of older people. Indeed, in a recent review of that book I complimented him on being himself an exemplar of an older person finding his purpose in life being ever renewed.

Now within a few further months he has produced this second book which deals with the ethical dilemmas involved in end-of-life issues, such as euthanasia, assisted dying and the despair that might lead to suicide, as seen through a Biblical lens. The author is fully aware of the current legal positions in many countries, the varied historical and social contexts of the books of the Bible, and the different interpretations that can be put upon their words, and he shares his extensive knowledge with the reader in a very accessible way. He rightly surmises that we will all face end-of-life issues and, without pressing his own views, hopes that his study may help us to come to our own conclusions. Far from being abstract and remote it is truly existential.

Dr Lowis does not avoid the really difficult questions that will affect our freedom to make moral decisions, such as whether our lives are pre-determined anyway and whether God's "offer of salvation" is exclusive to some or truly universal. This gives some context to his final chapter that offers a succinct and helpful summary of the attitudes of other world religions and of humanists to end-of-life issues.

The early chapters are a necessary prelude to the detailed study of all the relevant Biblical references in chapters 9 and 10, which are helpfully tabulated. To have accomplished so much in such a short book is truly impressive and provides us with a rich source of guidance in our ultimate ethical decisions.

Rev Dr Albert Jewell

Visiting Research Fellow
at Glyndwr University

PREFACE

EXPLORING ISSUES RELATING TO suicide, euthanasia and despair may on the face of it seem to be a very morbid pursuit, but this book is certainly not intended as such. In fact, the message that emerges is more one of hope, faith and perseverance in the face of difficulty, than one of gloom, doom and capitulation. Thus, it is hoped that the readers will not only be interested in reading what the Bible has to say about people in difficult situations, who despair and wonder if they can continue, but will also gain strength and inspiration that may help them if they are ever faced with such a distressing scenario. However, the intention is not to prescribe, but to just provide some evidence on which the reader can draw as an aid to making up his or her own mind. There can never be an ultimate right or wrong in any ethical dilemma but, the more informed we are, then the more likely we will be to make decisions that we shall not regret in the years to come.

This book aims to do more than just explore pertinent biblical texts. The Bible was written a long time ago, in a variety of historical, political, and cultural settings that are very different to what we have today, especially in the western hemisphere. All we have now are manuscripts that have been copied and translated many times, and with opportunities for errors to be made at each step. Is it any wonder, therefore, that scholars often disagree on how a particular passage should be interpreted, and applied in a contemporary situation? It would indeed be presumptuous for me to even attempt to impose on the reader any dogmatic explanation of the texts cited in this enquiry. Instead, in order to help put the quoted passages in context, I have included chapters that provide some background on the origins of each of the biblical books that are used, including the likely authorship, the purpose, and the date it was written.

Additional chapters then discuss the differences in the way scholars have attempted to interpret the Bible, such as by taking the message literally, compared with regarding it as an allegory for something else. Even if one is reasonably confident that a correct understanding of the guidance offered by a text has been achieved, another very pertinent question still needs to be considered. This is: do we in fact have the free will to take our own decisions, or is everything already predetermined by God? A further issue related to this is: do the actions we carry out in this world affect our standing with God in the next world? Put another way, are we all predestined to be saved regardless of our actions—the tenet of Universalism, or only some—the tenet of Particularism or, alternatively, does salvation depend on what we do in this life?

Before concentrating on the exploration of specific texts that have been suggested as relevant to end-of-life or despairing situations, I have included a chapter on the various types of guidance, laws, and exhortations that appear in the Bible, and their relevance to taking ethical decisions today. My aim with these preliminary chapters was to suitably prepare the reader for the unpacking of the biblical texts that are presented and discussed in the chapters that follow. It will be much more meaningful for the reader if he or she can formulate his or her own interpretation and understanding of the Bible passages, than to have them prescribed by somebody else. At the end of the day, if *you* are faced with a dilemma so desperate that it could possibly result in the decision to end a life prematurely, *you* will need to be confident that you have made the correct decision based on the best possible understanding of any advice you have been given.

Because this investigation is based on the Christian Bible, the findings are obviously more relevant to Christians than they are to those of other faiths (or none), although the Old Testament message is also the holy book of Judaism. In order to broaden the perspective, however, I have included a final chapter that presents a brief history of some non-Christian faiths and of humanism, and the views of spokespersons from these faiths on four key questions relating to the premature ending of a life. Whilst there is a high degree of overlap on many points, some interesting differences are revealed.

I have carried out many research studies over the years, and on a great variety of topics, both religious and secular. My training in both the biological and the social sciences has instilled into me the importance of avoiding presuppositions and any other biases, when carrying out such investigations. It is so easy to start off with a particular point of view, and then conduct research with the hope of obtaining results that confirm that same view. This serves no purpose at all, and good research obeys the principle of formulating an hypothesis that can be falsified—in other words, the outcome can be either what one proposes, *or* the opposite. This idea was propounded by the Austrian-British philosopher Karl Popper (1902–94), who believed that generalizations can never be completely verified, because contrary evidence might exist and be awaiting discovery. I discuss this in more detail in a 2004 paper.[1]

Popper's principle is followed by all serious researchers. Thus, the present investigation was carried out with a completely open mind as to what may emerge. Not only is it concerned with ethical guidance on matters specifically relating to ending a life before its natural time, but it also uncovers many biblical examples that give hope and courage to those who despair, and feel helpless in the face of life's difficulties. Although I have drawn some conclusions from this investigation myself, the book should provide sufficient background and detail for you, the reader, to form your own view. The exercise was a journey for me, with an unknown destination until I arrived, and I hope this will also be the case for you.

Dr Michael J. Lowis

Northampton, UK

June, 2015.

1. Lowis, "A Novel Methodology to Study the Propensity to Appreciate Music."

ACKNOWLEDGEMENTS

I wish to thank Rev Dr Albert Jewell for his valuable help with copy editing the manuscript, writing the Forward, and offering a number of helpful comments. I am also grateful to the representatives of several of the world religions and Humanists who provided responses to the questionnaire discussed in the final chapter.

INTRODUCTION
An Ethical Dilemma

WHAT WOULD WE DO if someone very close to us had a terminal illness, was in chronic pain with no hope of recovery, and pleaded with us to find a way to help them end their life so that they could be at peace? No doubt we all hope that we will never be faced with such a dilemma, torn on the one hand between seeing a loved one suffer so much and, on the other, believing that it is wrong to end a life prematurely. If we our self happened to be that person who was suffering, would we believe we had the right to decide our own destiny, and whether or not we should take our own life? There can be few, if any, dilemmas greater than these, but is there any guidance we can draw on to help us come to a decision? Even the law of the land can be circumvented by those determined enough, for example by travelling to a country where euthanasia is legal. Therefore, it is the ethical principle of right or wrong that needs to be resolved before we would even contemplate taking the matter further.

One resource to which many will turn is the Bible. Thus, the main aim of the present book is to search out and interpret the texts that may offer guidance for those who despair, and who contemplate ending the life of either themself or another before its natural time. Whilst an attempt will be made to draw conclusions that may help with this dilemma, the ultimate decision will inevitably remain with the individual concerned.

Whilst suicide and euthanasia both relate to facilitating the premature, unnatural ending of a human life, their definitions are somewhat different. One dictionary (2001)[1] defines suicide as: "the act of killing oneself intentionally; a person who kills himself or herself intentionally". J. P. Moreland (1991)[2] is more specific and suggests that it is an act that intentionally and directly causes one's own death as an ultimate end in itself, without coercion. This would differentiate it from an act of self-sacrifice carried out for the sake of others, even though it does involve the intentional taking of one's own life when this could have been avoided. In similar vein, it would also exclude the special circumstances of martyrdom, whereby a person also freely ends his or her life, or accepts that it be terminated, but this time it is for God and one's religious beliefs.

With regard to euthanasia, the dictionary definition is: "the act or practice of putting painlessly to death, especially in cases of incurable suffering; an easy mode of death".[3] This can only be regarded as an "umbrella" definition, as commentators have identified a range of actions that can be subsumed under this heading. Most variants are accommodated by the comprehensive scheme of Keith Essex (2000),[4] namely: passive—with the subdivisions "voluntary", "involuntary" and "non-voluntary", and active—with the same three sub-divisions, but in this case divided still further into "direct" and "indirect" categories. Whilst active euthanasia involves the deliberate administration of substances that are intended to cause death, the passive type entails withholding treatment that would sustain life. The voluntary category in each case applies when the patient specifically requests the procedure, involuntary where he or she does not, and non-voluntary occurs when the patient's wishes are unknown.

It is clear that any discussion on voluntary assisted dying, whether it is by one's own hand, or with the help of another, cannot rely on a simple catch-all definition and therefore a black and white conclusion. For example, the most passive means of assisted dying is probably the switching off of life support machines, and

1. *Chambers Dictionary*, 1674.
2. Moreland, "The Morality of Suicide," 218.
3. *Chambers Dictionary*, 558.
4. Essex, "Euthanasia," 201.

this procedure is now widely accepted, subject to specific conditions. At the other end of the scale, the act of one person administering a lethal medication to another remains highly controversial, and is subject to criminal proceedings in many countries. However, if one person prepares such a lethal potion for another, who then self-administers it to intentionally end his or her own life, this is commonly referred to as assisted suicide. If the medication is wholly administered to the recipient by another person, then this would be euthanasia regardless of whether it was voluntary or involuntary. When we turn to the Bible to seek specific and unambiguous guidance in this matter, we encounter similar difficulties because such texts that do relate to end of life issues are subject to a range of interpretations.

Referring again to the dictionary,[5] ethics is defined as a system of morals or rules of human behavior, and morals are defined as being related to conduct considered good or evil.[6] This, of course, begs the question of how to define good and evil behavior. Whole books have been devoted to trying to arrive at a satisfying answer to this, and the present volume is not intended to contribute to this debate. Rather, it concentrates more narrowly on how the Bible can provide guidance on the specific topics of suicide, euthanasia and despair.

J. L. Houlden (1979)[7] states that the overriding principle of biblical ethics is the love of God that we should share with our brothers: "We love because he first loved us." (1 John 4:19) (all quotations from New International Version [NIV] unless otherwise stated). However, he cautions that the writers wrote in their own contexts and were not faced with many of the issues that we have today. Arthur Holmes' (1984)[8] view concurs, with his comment that biblical guidance is not exhaustive, especially on contemporary issues, and he raises the pertinent question of whether or not moral beliefs and practices vary with culture ("cultural rela-

5. *Chambers Dictionary,* 554.

6. Ibid., 1047–48.

7. Houlden, *Ethics and the New Testament,* 39.

8. Holmes, *Ethics: Approaching Moral Decisions.*

tivism"). His own conclusion is that the Christian ethic is deonto-logical, and that all moral principles are therefore universal: divine law is the paradigm ("universalism"). A succinct statement on the moral guidance to be found in the New Testament is offered by Richard Longenecker (1984),[9] with his exhortation to place stress on God's free and sovereign encounter through his Spirit, and to ask what the loving thing to do is.

Whilst specific statements on ethical principles are contained in both the Old and New Testaments, as will be discussed in later chapters, not all scholars agree that the two volumes have equal relevance, even though the Alexandrian Church Father Origen (185–254 AD) believed that there was harmony between them.[10] There are 613 laws cited in Deuteronomy, and Christopher Wright comments that Moses supplemented the original Decalogue to guide the Israelites as they entered the Promised Land. Commonly known as "The Law", Mark Biddle (2003)[11] suggests that these are not meant to be a set of restricted rules, but as guidance for living a life as the people of God. From the universal principle, one needs to deduce what is the right thing to do to resolve a particular issue; this usually requires some specific action.[12]

Larry Pettegrew (2000)[13] comments that God's glory is the goal of ethics, and that the Bible's ethical direction takes five forms: what is prohibited, what is permitted, what we are commanded to do, precedents, and actions that are condoned by praise. To give just one example, of a "command" that may be relevant to the topic of assisted-dying: "let us be good to all people . . . " (Gal 6:10). How seriously should Christians keep the law of the Old Testament? According to Gordon Fee and Douglas Stuart (2001),[14] we are not obliged to do so unless the law is renewed in the New Covenant. Jesus does refer back to the old laws from time to time, and is quite

---

9. Longenecker, *New Testament Social Ethics for Today.*
10. Wright, "The Ethical Authority of the Old Testament."
11. Biddle, *Deuteronomy.*
12. Butler, "Ethics," 204–6.
13. Pettegrew, "Theology and the Basis of Ethics."
14. Fee and Stuart, *How to Read the Bible for all its Worth.*

specific when asked which the greatest commandment is. He responds that all the laws of the prophets hang on the exhortations to love the Lord, and to love one's neighbor (Matt 22:37-40).

Having now established the main parameters, as mentioned in the opening paragraph the remainder of this book will examine what the Bible has to say on the matter of suicide, euthanasia and coping with despair, what conclusions may be drawn from this, and how these may guide us in our decisions should the need ever arise. The enquiry will be conducted in an open-minded way, without presuppositions, and will be as much a journey for the writer as it is hoped it will be for the reader.

CHAPTER 1

THE CURRENT LEGAL POSITION

A TRAWL OF REPORTS in the news media and on the World Wide Web at the end of the year 2014, revealed that assisted dying was very much a current issue, and that public opinion was becoming more accepting of the right to die with dignity at a time that one chooses. Cases have also been reported in the press of individuals killing their seriously ill, and often elderly, partner to prevent further suffering, even though the law as it stands regards this as murder. Keith Essex (2000)[1] reports that in the USA there has been a swing toward those in favor of voluntary euthanasia with, at that time of writing, the support being about 60–75 percent. By the year 2014, several countries had reached a decision on the legalization of assisted suicide and euthanasia. Under carefully defined conditions, this is currently legal in Albania, Columbia, Germany, Japan and Switzerland. Whilst not legal throughout the whole of the United States of America, it is permitted in the states of Montana, New Mexico, Oregon, Vermont and Washington. Active assisted suicide is legal only in Belgium, Netherlands and Luxemburg, although the passive procedures are more widely tolerated throughout the world.

It is pertinent here to mention the influential work of Dr Jack Kevorkian, a physician in the USA who became know in some circles as "Dr Death" for his work on assisted suicide. His story is

---

1. Essex, "Euthanasia," 191.

detailed by Neil Nicol and Harry Wylie (2006).[2] Anguished by observing slow and agonizing deaths, Kevorkian devised a machine that could be operated by a patient to self-administer lethal medication. He would only make the necessary arrangements subject to compliance with very strict and detailed protocols that ensured the patient was fully aware of what he or she was doing, and why. His first such assisted suicide occurred in Oregon in 1989, after which he immediately informed the police and was arrested, but was ultimately released without charge as there was no law applicable to assisted suicide.

Kevorkian continued with his procedure over the next decade or so, enabling over 130 people to die with dignity. He was brought to trial on several occasions, and welcomed the opportunity to publicize his views, but he managed to evade conviction. Evade, that is, until he attempted to push the boundaries further by administering the lethal medication to the patient himself rather than by the previous self-medication procedure. This time he was found guilty of murder and, in 1999, was sentenced to long-term imprisonment.

Dr Kevorkian's well publicized activities stirred up public opinion, especially in his home state. In the year 1994 the USA State of Oregon passed by a small majority the "Death with dignity act". However, an injunction was immediately placed against it but this was lifted three years later when the residents had the opportunity to vote on it. The measure was approved, with 60 percent voting in favor.[3] Under the act, patients with a terminal illness that will kill them within six months may request a lethal dose of medication for self-administration only, providing they are aged eighteen or over, and are mentally competent. The detailed protocol includes the stipulation that two witnesses must confirm the request, and that the medical records must be examined by a second physician. Participation in this action by the physicians, pharmacists and other health workers is voluntary.

2. Nicol and Wylie, *Between the Dying and the Dead.*
3. Ibid., 199–200.

The Netherlands became the first country to legalize what we can now term "voluntary active euthanasia", when it expanded a 1984 Supreme Court ruling that doctors would be free from prosecution from complying with requests for euthanasia in terms of the "Termination of Life on Request and Assisted Suicide (Review Procedures) Act" in 2002. The Netherlands Government website reports that a set of stringent control procedures, similar to that of the Oregon law, must be followed, including an examination after the event by a special review committee. A significant requirement that differs from most other examples, including the Oregon one, is that the lethal medication is administered only by a physician.[4]

More recently, the BBC reported that on 6th February, 2015, Canada's Supreme Court ruled that doctors may help patients who have severe and incurable medical conditions to die. The case was brought by a civil rights group, and the nine judges were unanimous in their decision. They stated that the current ban, which was introduced in the year 1993, infringed the life, liberty, and security of its citizens. The Canadian government now has a year to draft new legislation that recognizes the rights of the individual in such matters but, until then, the ban remains with a maximum penalty of fourteen years for infringement.[5]

For countries like the United Kingdom, where euthanasia is currently illegal, individuals who desire to end their existence because of extreme medical conditions, have to travel to countries where their life can be legally terminated in appropriate circumstances. Such an opportunity exists in Switzerland through the organization "Dignitas". Their information website[6] states that Dignitas was founded in May, 1998 at Forch, near Zurich, and pursues no commercial interests. It has "the objective of ensuring a life and death with dignity for its members and of allowing other people to benefit from these values."

Dignitas offers a number of services, but pertinent among them is that, "in the case of medically diagnosed hopeless or

4. "Euthanasia, Overview."
5. "Canada to Allow Doctor-assisted Suicide."
6. "Dignitas, Our Service."

incurable illnesses, unbearable pain or unendurable disabilities (it) offers its members the option of an accompanied suicide." The procedure is that the patient is handed a lethal, oral medication for self-administration. This complies with the Swiss law that states "anyone who helps someone to commit suicide, providing they are not acting out of selfish motives, cannot be punished." The organization "Exit" in Switzerland reported that 583 people were helped by them to die in 2014, an increase from 459 in the year 2013. A statement from Dignitas said that 244 Britons had made the journey to die since the year 2002.[7]

In the UK, a bill was tabled in The House of Lords to legalize euthanasia, and this achieved its second reading late in 2014. In January 2015 this was again debated in the Lords, but it was accepted that there was then insufficient time within the life of the current parliament to progress this through the House of Commons. It will therefore have to be tabled again after the general election in May 2015. This "Assisted dying bill", introduced by Lord Falconer, applies to terminally ill adults who are judged to have no more than six months to live and who comply with a detailed protocol that includes time to reflect. Medical intervention would be restricted to preparing a lethal medication and the means to self-administer it. Thus, as with the Oregon and Dignitas procedures, the individual will have been helped to take his or her own life, but will not have been euthanized by a second party.[8]

Inevitably, controversy has accompanied this bill in its journey thus far through the legislative process, and at the time of writing it is not known what the final outcome will be. According to a news article by Ella Rhodes in the British professional journal *The Psychologist,* (2014)[9] whilst some 80 percent of the general public is in favor of the bill, apparently many psychologists are not. This last comment prompted a robust response in the October and November issues from psychologists who supported the bill, including an acknowledgement of the contribution of their profession in

---

7. "Assisted Dying at Swiss Clinic."

8. "Assisted Dying Bill (HL)."

9. Rhodes, "We Should Bring Death back to Life," 648–49.

providing appropriate support for the terminally ill. There were, however, only two scant references to religious considerations.

This imbalance prompted a letter from the present writer that was published in the December edition of the journal, urging health practitioners not to shy away from faith issues when faced with providing advice on end of life matters. It was happenstance that a women currently suffering from Stage lll cancer saw one of the journals, and wrote in to say that, knowing that death was near, she would be delighted to receive enough morphine to help her on her way.

The discussion so far has been about active euthanasia or assisted suicide, where individuals are supplied with the means to end their own lives by a qualified medical practitioner. However, passive euthanasia, for example turning off life support mechanisms, is more widely accepted and practiced. Whilst rarely openly admitted, other passive means to hasten the end of life of the terminally ill are sometimes used in the UK, and probably also elsewhere. These include withholding nutrition, and administering more pain killers than are necessary.

A case in point concerns "The Liverpool Care Pathway", introduced during the 1990s to save patients from often painful invasive testing and treatment that offered no chance of preventing death, but were just aimed at prolonging life. The pathway was intended to be "passive", and with the full consent of relatives. It involved the withdrawal of life-saving and life support measures, the administration of sedation, and often the withholding of nutrition and hydration. Death usually followed in a little over twenty-four hours. However, following reports of abuse of the system, in 2003 the Department of Health issued a statement saying that the Pathway would be phased out and replaced with an individual approach to end of life care.

This review of the current legality of suicide and euthanasia was neither intended to be exhaustive, nor to report in detail on the practices employed in all countries. Rather it was to highlight the growing demand for people to be able to take decisions both with regard to their own death, and to avoid standing by helplessly whilst a loved one suffers without hope of a medical cure. Indeed, as mentioned earlier, some individuals are so desperate that they take the law into their own hands and either make the journey to a country where euthanasia is legal, or even personally help someone they care about to die. Despite this being currently illegal in the UK, judges often exercise discretion and compassion and resist imposing punitive sanctions on those involved. Letters and articles, both for and against voluntary euthanasia, continue to appear in the British press at regular intervals, and it is clear that the issue remains a divisive one.

With regard to self-administered suicide without the involvement of another person, this was viewed as a very serious breach of acceptable behavior in Britain in the Middle Ages, and it was forbidden to give a Christian burial to suicide victims. In fact, suicide was illegal, and those who survived the attempt were taken before the courts. It was only in the year 1961 that suicide ceased to be a crime in Britain. The UK Office of National Statistics reported that the suicide rate in this country rose significantly from 11.1 per 100,000 of the population in the year 2010, to 11.8 in 2011. The rate was over three times higher for males than it was for females, but the overall incidence was still lower than the peak of 14.9 per 100,000 in the year 1981.[10]

Thus the issue of prematurely ending a life, whether it be one's own or that of another at their request, remains divisive and controversial; it cannot be ignored and needs to be addressed.

10. "Suicides in the United Kingdom."

CHAPTER 2

THE OLD TESTAMENT AS EVIDENCE

BEFORE IDENTIFYING AND ANALYZING the biblical texts that can help inform on the ethics of suicide, euthanasia, and despair, it is prudent to first review just how reliable the scriptures are likely to be as evidence, including the extent that they can be regarded as inerrant. This will be followed by a summary of what is known about the origins, authors, and purposes of the Old Testament sources used in this enquiry. The following two chapters will then review similar details for the New Testament sources used.

None of the original texts ("autographs") of either Testament have ever been found, and it is doubtful that they ever will be. Thus we have to rely on the earliest available copies, which themselves might be copies of an unknown succession of even earlier copies. Each time this is done there is opportunity for error. A comparison of examples of different copies of the same text confirms that such scribing errors could easily occur. Sometimes the copyists edited the manuscripts, either in a misguided attempt to clarify the meaning as they saw it, or for political reasons to comply with their own ideologies. Add to this the problems with translations from old Hebrew, Greek or sometimes Aramaic into our own preferred modern language, sometimes involving discretion by the translator to try and convey the original idea. Thus it is no surprise that considerable skill is needed to try and tease out what the original text was intended to convey to the audience at that time, in the pertaining historical, cultural, social and political milieu.

The oldest reasonably complete biblical manuscript yet found is the Codex Sinaiticus, which is written in Greek and dates from the fourth century AD. It is housed in the British Museum in London. The Codex Vaticanus is from a similar period, and it is kept in the Vatican Library in Rome. Several other manuscripts date from the fifth century and later, including for example the codices Alexandrianus (British Museum), Ephraemi (Bibliothèque Nationale, Paris), and Bezae (Cambridge University Library).

Scholars agree that Old Testament history begins about 2,000 BC when Abraham was believed to have entered Canaan, but it is unlikely that these stories were written down until at least five hundred years later. The first five books—the Pentateuch, also known as the Torah—are held by many to have been written by Moses around 1405 to 1445 BC, with the earlier events having being preserved and passed down through oral tradition. The Hebrew texts were translated into Greek in about 250 BC and are referred to as the Septuagint (LXX). In an attempt to obtain a standard text, Jewish scholars—the Masorites, working from the ninth to the fifteenth century AD—compared all known manuscripts, and produced the Masoretic Text (MT).

The task of establishing the true facts, let alone the intended meaning, of any of the biblical accounts remains a challenging task for exegetical scholars and interpreters. Even then, just as the authors wrote from their own viewpoints, today's interpreters sometimes struggle to avoid being influenced by their own presuppositions and biases. Interpretation will be influenced by the extent to which a scholar accepts that the biblical writings directly express the words of God himself (i.e. the extent to which they are inerrant). Did God dictate every word, or were the texts composed by human beings imbibed to a greater or lesser extent with Divine knowledge? Some believe that we cannot regard the scriptures as error free, but we can accept them as an infallible guide to living one's faith.

There is no universal agreement on this. The conservative view can be summarized with James Hamilton's (2010)[1] statement that "the . . . books of the Protestant canon are inspired by the Holy Spirit and are therefore inerrant". In other words, they are totally true and trustworthy. To support this, he cites a number of Bible passages including 2 Tim 3:16–17 ("all scripture is breathed out by God"), 2 Pet 1:20–21 ("and men spoke from God"), and Prov 30:5 ("Every word of God proves true"). There are, in addition, references that specifically report God's actual spoken word, for example: "The Lord commanded Moses to tell the people" (Lev 4:1); "Moses spoke and God answered him with thunder" (Ex 19:19) and, in the New Testament: "a voice from the cloud said 'This is my own dear son'" (Matt 17:5).

At the opposite pole are the liberals, who see everything as subjective and open to interpretation, and that the Bible is basically an account of the religious experiences of some people in the past, rather than something in which God and the Holy Spirit had direct influence. Millard Erickson (1985)[2] would regard this as "intuition theory", which holds that the inspiration of the scripture writers is no different from that of other great religious and philosophical thinkers, without the need for any divine involvement. Although Jesus often cited the authority of the scriptures (that is, the Old Testament), and is quoted as saying "We know that what the scripture says is true for ever" (John 10:35), he still found the need to interpret texts for his audience, usually commencing "It is written . . . but I say to you."

Examples include Jesus predicting Peter's denial and stating "I will strike the shepherd, and the sheep of the flock will be scattered" (Matt 26:31) which is an interpretation of Zechariah 13:7, and "It is written: 'Man shall not live by bread alone'" (Luke 4:4) which is a quotation from Deuteronomy 8:3. In Matthew 11:10 Jesus explains that John the Baptist is "the one about whom it was written", and continues with a quotation from Malachi 3:1. A little

---

1. Hamilton, *Still Sola Scriptura*, 217.
2. Erickson, *Christian Theology*, 206.

later (12:3) he asks his disciples "Haven't you read what David did when his companions were hungry?" This refers to Leviticus 24:9.

Some confidence in the reliability of the biblical texts can be gained from the fact that the books of the canon as we have it today were only accepted after much deliberation. The final selection was based on an acknowledgement that the writer was a prophet who had directly heard the word of God (Old Testament), or that he was an eyewitness of the resurrected Jesus, or was under the authority of such a person (New Testament). An anonymous writer in *Bibliotheca Sacra* (1914)[3] examined the reliability of biblical evidence based on the principles of jurisprudence, the science that deals with the competency of what is proposed as evidence. The writer concluded that the Bible can be legally regarded as a properly preserved "ancient document", and therefore the eyewitness reports, being accurately recorded, are admissible as evidence.

With reference to the Old Testament sources, eleven of these books include texts that provide some guidance on coping with life's difficulties severe enough to lead some to seek an end to it all, as well as describing some actual deaths. The intention in the present chapter is to provide some general background on the biblical sources that have been found helpful in this quest; specific examples and texts will be cited in later chapters. The books will be reviewed in the order they appear in the Bible.

As mentioned above, Exodus, being one of the books of the Pentateuch, was thought to have been written by Moses. However, it is accepted that some passages were added after Moses' death. As is suggested by the title, this book describes the exodus of the Israelites from Egypt, led by Moses, but it includes the giving of the Ten Commandments at Sinai. Tremper Longman and Raymond Dillard[4] state that traditionally the date of the exodus, and therefore the book, is for a time during the fifteenth century BC. If the passage in 1 Kings 6:1 that refers to an event 480 years after the Israelites left Egypt is accepted, then the date can be narrowed

---

3. "We should Bring Death Back to Life," 648–49.

4. Longman and Dillard, "Exodus," 65–9.

to about 1447 BC. Some scholars dispute the traditional date and believe that it should be two or three hundred years later.

T. D. Alexander (2007)[5] notes that the main themes in Exodus, in addition to the journey itself, are about knowing God through personal experience, and the making of the covenant that obliges the Israelites to live by the law as recorded in the Decalogue. Pertinent to the present enquiry on ethical issues, the book also emphasizes the need for the Israelites to follow the moral imperatives of compassion and justice.

The next source is the book of Numbers, also one of the Pentateuch and, therefore, the same observations on date and author apply as per Exodus. This text continues the narrative of the journey to the Promised Land, but it also includes many additional laws that must be followed. Much emphasis is placed on the earlier covenant that God made with Abraham, when the Israelites were blessed and the land of Canaan was promised. However, the people were apparently often discouraged with the on-going hardship, constantly complaining and rebelling against God, despite Moses' best efforts to keep control. Notwithstanding this weakness, God maintains his presence among the people, guiding them and keeping his commitment to bring them to the Promised Land.

The same comments on authorship apply to the book of Deuteronomy, which describes the final stage of the exodus and the preparations to enter the Promised Land. The Israelites would be subject to great challenges as well as pagan influences. It was timely that Moses led the people in a covenant renewal before the conquest began.[6] He reminds them that God will continue to bless them, and help them during their forthcoming challenges, as he had done during their forty-year journey. In return they must remain faithful to him, and obey the many laws that have been established to preserve welfare and justice.

The next three books used in the present study were written a little later than the Pentateuch, the first during the pre-monarchic period (approximately 1000–1500 BC) and the third during the

5. Alexander, "Exodus," 92–120.

6. Craige, *The book of Deuteronomy.*

early years of the monarchy. The book of Judges relates stories about local military leaders or "judges", which occurred shortly after the invasion of Canaan, and is traditionally held to have been written by the prophet Samuel, who may have lived sometime around the eleventh century BC. Barry Webb (2011)[7] states that this book appears to have been based on source material contemporary with the events described. However, it might have been part of one long piece of historical writing that was completed during the sixth century BC and later divided into seven separate books. Tremper Longman and Raymond Dillard[8] mention that, despite the sin and rebellion of the people, God declared that he would not abandon them and that he was always ready to save his chosen people if they repented and returned to him.

The first book of Samuel describes the transition from the period of the judges to that of the monarchy heralded by King Saul (1043–1011 BC). Although traditionally the prophet Samuel has been held to be the author, David Payne (2011)[9] states that he could not have been, because chapter 27, verse six shows knowledge of the divided kingdom that occurred in 950 BC ("So on that day, Achish gave [David] him Ziklag, and it has belonged to the Kings of Judah ever since"), which would have been at least fifty years after Samuel's death. The book continues to relate the Deuteronomic history, and makes the point that remaining faithful to God brings success, but disobedience brings disaster. However, under God's laws, the rights of all people must be preserved. The second book of Samuel continues the historical narrative, largely devoted to the reign of King David who, although far from perfect, was a man of deep faith and devotion to God. The author is unknown but, for the reasons mentioned earlier, is unlikely to be the prophet of the same name, and the date of writing was probably after the king's death in 970 BC.

The first book of Kings is the next to be cited, which records the death of David, the reign of Solomon, and the division of the

7. Webb, "Judges," 261–86.

8. Longman and Dillard, "Judges," 133.

9. Payne, "1 and 2 Samuel," 296–333.

kingdom into Israel (north) and Judah (south). Many kings reigned during the subsequent three hundred or more years, most of them bad but with a few who tried to return their country to a state of loyalty to God and obedience to his laws. Whilst Jewish tradition holds that the prophet Jeremiah was the author, others doubt this and suggest it was by an anonymous writer exiled in Babylon.[10] John Bimson (2011)[11] suggests a date of writing between 561 and 538 BC as most likely, because the latter date coincides with the first return of Jewish exiles to Jerusalem. He adds that, just like the era of the judges had failed, so now did the monarchy. Notwithstanding this, God remained committed to Israel—he remains active in grace as well as judgment. Even though the people are in exile, God may forgive them if they now repent and seek him.

The author of the book of Job is anonymous, but it is thought to have been penned by an Israelite, although with possible later additions. There is, however, a suggestion that Job was not a real person, but that the suffering ascribed to him was intended to be symbolic of that of the Jews at the time of the exile.[12] Although the plot refers to an earlier period in Israel's history, the book was probably written later, with suggestions ranging from the fourth to the seventh centuries BC (Butler, 2001).[13] Job writes about the hardships he had to endure but did not deserve, and he takes God to task over what he regards as unjustifiable treatment. In response, God describes his creative power and wisdom, and that he still controls the world through good times and bad. Job regrets his complaints, and accepts God's judgments. In return, God ensures that Job attains prosperity again.

The book of Psalms is cited seven times in this enquiry, more than any other book in either Testament. There are one hundred and fifty psalms, divided into five groups. They were composed by various authors over a period of time, and the genres include hymns of praise and worship, thanksgiving, prayers for help and

10. Longman and Dillard, "Kings," 168.

11. Bimson, "1 and 2 Kings," 334–87.

12. Clines, "Job," 459–84.

13. Butler, "Job," 360–61.

salvation, and pleas for forgiveness. At least some were used by Jesus, and are quoted by several of the New Testament writers. J. A. Motyer (2011)[14] states that it used to be fashionable to date many psalms to the first century BC but, more recently, there is a willingness to ascribe dates a millennium further back to the King's period. The themes suggested by Motyer for the psalms cited in this enquiry include: distress transformed by prayer (Psalm 13); righteousness is no guarantee of a trouble-free life but the Lord sides with us against our opponents (34); counter morbid thoughts about the transience of life by turning to God (90); overcoming anguish and entering the gates of righteousness (118); prayers were answered for David so that he rejoiced (138); God is all-knowing, all-present, and all-creating (139); and, the Lord is all the security and enrichment his people need (147).

Ecclesiastes may seem to be a pessimistic work to include in an enquiry about coping with end of life issues and despair, but its sentiments are those to which people can relate. Yes, life is grim, but it would be much worse without God to whom we ultimately have to give an account; we must fear him and keep his commandments. Solomon is traditionally credited with the authorship, inter alia on the strength of the first verse that states the words were written by the philosopher who was David's son, king in Jerusalem; but not all agree. If it was Solomon, this would date the book to the tenth century BC, but it is likely to have been edited and updated, with a final version being created in the fifth century.[15]

The book of Jonah, perhaps best known for its narrative of a man being swallowed by a large fish, contains no indication of the author or the date of composition. However, Longman and Dillard (2007)[16] state that Jonah, the main character, was in fact a real prophet who lived during the reign of Jeroboam ll (786–746 BC). The book is a narrative about the leading character, who tried to disobey God's command to go to Nineveh but, eventually, reluctantly agreed to do so. The main message concerns God's love and

---

14. Motyer, "Psalms," 485–583.

15. Longman and Dillard, "Ecclesiastes," 278–88.

16. Longman and Dillard, "Jonah," 443–48.

mercy, even toward the enemies of his people. Despite a suggestion that Jonah was not a person, but was intended to symbolize the "swallowing up" of Israel during the time of captivity, and the challenges faced after the return from exile, Jonah and Nineveh are mentioned by Jesus: ". . . the sign of the prophet Jonah . . . The men of Nineveh will stand up at the judgment . . ." (Matt 12:39–41, paralleled in Luke 11:29–30).

The author of the final Old Testament book to be used, Jeremiah, is widely accepted to be the prophet of the same name, whose life spanned the end of the seventh and beginning of the sixth centuries BC. However, some believe there may have been others who added to the text. Jeremiah's main mission was to warn the nation of Judah of the threat of invasion, and to denounce corruption, idolatry, and apostasy.[17] He urged a return to the old covenant and to ignore the words of false prophets. His warning went unheeded, and Judah was invaded by the Babylonians in 597 BC. Despite this grave situation, Jeremiah preaches that God will not abandon them and that he will eventually restore both Israel and Judah. Moreover, God will write a new covenant on the hearts of his people, and Jeremiah foretells of the messianic hope for the future which, by implication, is the coming of Jesus.

17. Harrison, *Jeremiah and Lamentations*.

CHAPTER 3

THE GOSPELS, ACTS, AND
REVELATION AS EVIDENCE

THE NEW TESTAMENT BOOKS were, of course, penned more recently, being mostly written in Greek during the first century AD,
in the Middle-eastern world of Judaism when Judah was part of the
Roman Empire. Thus, whilst the time lag is less than that for the
Old Testament, and in particular for the Pentateuch, as discussed
in the previous chapter, it is unlikely that any of the original texts
were written down at the time of the happenings they describe. It is
more likely that they were passed on by oral tradition, or retained
in the memories of the witnesses for thirty years or more, before
they were documented. This chapter is concerned with reviewing
the authorship, dates, and purpose of the gospels, and the books
of Acts and Revelation, and the following chapter will review the
Pauline and other epistles used in this enquiry.

The gospel of Matthew is generally attributed to the disciple
of that name, who would thus have had first-hand knowledge of
Jesus and his activities. Matthew's recruitment is described in his
own gospel (9:9); he was seen sitting at a tax collector's booth and
responded to Jesus' call to follow him. He is named as one of the
twelve a little further on (10:3), and also in Mark 3:18, Luke 6:15,
and Acts 1:13. Matthew's recruitment story is paralleled in Mark
2:14 and Luke 5:27, but here he is named as Levi, with the latter
adding "son of Alphaeus." In his discussion on the authorship of

this gospel, Craig Keener (1997)[1] states that some scholars remain to be convinced, and mention that Matthew's use of Mark casts some doubt on the former being an eyewitness of the events he describes. However, no alternative names have been suggested.

There is lack of a consensus on the date this gospel was created, but Craig Keener[2] cites evidence for a post–70 AD date that includes Matthew's references to both the rabbinic and Pharisaism movements that only became prominent after this time, and his use of Mark (see above). However, others prefer a date as early as 62 AD or even before. Andy Woods (2007)[3] suggests that the gospel's Jewish content argues for its priority, since the early church was primarily Jewish and the text suggests that the writer had a Jewish audience in mind. For example, Matthew emphasizes Jesus' role as a teacher (e.g. "go and learn what this means" Matt 9:13) and he seeks to convince his readers that the Old Testament prophesies had been fulfilled in Jesus, that he was the messiah and, through him, the kingdom of God had "broken into" this world.[4] Notwithstanding this lack of certainty, Scott McKnight (1988)[5] favors the "Oxford hypothesis" that Matthew and Luke both drew on Mark's account (regarded by many as the earliest), and an earlier postulated document usually designated "Q".

Craig Keener (1997)[6] also suggests that Mathew's purpose was to counter the rhetoric of the Pharisaism and the emerging rabbinic movement, and to compile a "handbook" of Jesus' life and teaching for the Jewish Christian community. Richard France (2011)[7] adds that Matthew's book can be thought of as a "teaching gospel" as it contains stories and sayings of Jesus that bear on the regular concerns of church life. He notes that the writer's special interests are Jesus as the promised messiah anticipated by the

1. Keener, *Matthew*, 31–32.

2. Ibid., 33–34.

3. Woods, "Purpose of Matthew's Gospel," 5–19.

4. Van den Brink, "Commentary on the Gospel of Matthew."

5. McKnight, *Interpreting the Synoptic Gospels*, 36.

6. Keener, *Matthew*, 34–35.

7. France, "Matthew," 904–6.

Jewish people as fulfillment of the Old Testament prophesies, and Jesus the king who came to proclaim the kingship of God and his own role as the universal king.

As is stated right at the start of Mark's gospel, its purpose is to present the good news about Jesus the messiah. The author is anonymous, but he is commonly believed to be (John) Mark, son of Mary, in whose home in Jerusalem the believers met.[8] Acts Chapter 12 relates how Peter had just been helped by an angel to escape from prison, and verse twelve reads "he went to the house of Mary the mother of John, also called Mark, where many people had gathered and were praying." "John Mark" is also mentioned in Acts 12:25 and 15:37, and "Mark" is cited several times, including in Colossians 4:10 where he is referred to as the cousin of Barnabas, and as a travelling companion of both Paul and his cousin.

Mark was too young to have been an eye-witness of Jesus, but he probably lived in Jerusalem where he would have known many of Jesus' followers.[9] He was with Peter in Rome during the later years ("My son Mark", 1 Pet 5:13). Peter had declared that he would make every effort to ensure that a record was made of his experiences with Jesus (2 Pet 1:15), and Mark may have been the scribe who committed this to writing. This notion is supported by the discovery of a letter written by Clement of Alexandria in about 190 AD, which refers to Peter's notes being included in Mark's gospel.[10]

Most scholars date Mark's gospel to about 65–70 AD, and it could have been written around the time of Peter's death in about 64 AD. However, a minority of others have put forward arguments for either an earlier or later date. Even though Mark's book is placed second in the New Testament, because of this comparatively early date it is held my many (but not all) to have been the first of the gospels to be written.[11] [12] Donald Guthrie[13] considers

8. Moule, *The Gospel according to Mark*, 4–5.

9. Cole, "Mark," 946–47.

10. Moule, *Gospel according to Mark*.

11. Ibid.

12. Cole, "Mark," 946.

13. Guthrie, *New Testament Introduction*.

that Mark's contribution is essentially a factual account of the life of Jesus, which would make sense if it was a record of the facts as related by the disciple Peter. He also suggests that it was written for Gentiles in Rome, not only to proclaim the good news of Jesus, but also to encourage those who faced persecution. Alan Cole[14] adds that Mark was also endeavoring to show the Roman authorities that Christians posed no threat.

The third gospel and the book of Acts are generally agreed to have both been authored by a man called Luke. He was not an eyewitness to the events relating to Jesus but, as recorded in Luke 1:1–4, he carefully searched out evidence from other writers and witnesses in order to write an orderly account "of things that have been fulfilled." Luke was a cultured man who at times was a companion of Philip the evangelist as well as the apostle Paul—in fact he often uses the pronoun "we" (e.g. Acts 16:10)—so he would have had much opportunity to question his colleagues on the life of Jesus and the early church.[15] Morris also observes that Paul mentions various companions who had been with him, including Titus, Demas, Crescens, and Luke (2 Timothy, 4:9–11), and any of these could conceivably have been the author, although there is no reason for nominating anyone but Luke himself.

Trent Butler[16] notes that tradition holds that Luke was a Gentile physician, citing Paul's statement "Our dear friend Luke, the doctor" (Col 4:14). Additionally, Leon Morris[17] points to examples of medical language, including "*high* fever" (Luke, 4:38), and "*full of* leprosy" (5:12, NKJV). Scholars fail to agree on the date that these two books were written, and suggestions range from the early sixties AD to the first part of the second century. Morris[18] favors an early date and, in support of this, states that Acts ends with Paul in prison but there is no mention of his release and subsequent martyrdom. In addition, there are no references to the Pauline

14. Cole, "Mark," 946–77.
15. Morris, *Luke,* 16–28.
16. Butler, "Luke," 402–3.
17. Morris, *Luke,* 16–24.
18. Ibid., 24–28.

epistles, which would have been expected if the date was later, and that no event later than 62 AD is mentioned. However, the fact that Luke states that many have written before him (1:1) implies the existence of early writings that have yet to be discovered.

Donald Guthrie[19] refers to Luke dedicating his gospel to the "most excellent Theophilus" 1:3, and Luke also mentions this man in the first verse of Acts chapter 1. Guthrie suggests that Theophilus was a real person, possibly of some social standing, and clearly a Gentile. He adds that there is abundant evidence, such as Luke's universalism, that the most likely destination was a Gentile audience, possibly in Rome, who were interested in a historical account of Christianity.

It is believed that these three Synoptic Gospels, plus that of John (vide infra), had been collected as a canonical unit during the second half of the second century, as evidenced by the defense of the fourfold gospel canon by Irenaeus in 180 AD.[20]

The book of Acts can be regarded as a continuation of what was commenced in Luke's gospel, that being a history of the early church. Because these books comprise two parts of the same narrative, conclusions with regard to date of composition and target audience of Acts are similar to those offered for Luke. After a brief link with the last meeting with Jesus and his ascension, and a description of the beginnings of the church in Jerusalem, Judaea and Samaria, the narrative moves on to the conversion of Paul and his missionary journeys. It is the only first-century example of a history of the early church that we have, and Howard Marshall[21] opines that Acts was intended to be evangelistic, presenting an account of Christian beginnings in order to strengthen faith and give assurances that its foundation was firm.

Before moving on to the other main biblical sources on which the present book draws for evidence, mention should be made of the "synoptic problem". This is a term used to describe the study of, and attempted explanation of, the similarities and

19. Guthrie, *New Testament Introduction*, 95–6.

20. Butler, "Bible, Formation," 72–75.

21. Marshall, *Acts*, 17–21.

differences between the first three gospels. Questions raised by scholars include: which gospel was written first? Did some gospel writers borrow from the texts of others? Could there have been other sources, now lost, from which some or all of the writers drew? As already stated earlier, Luke specifically mentioned right at the start of his gospel that there were various sources that he consulted but, unfortunately, he does not identify them.

Scot McKnight[22] reviews the major solutions to the problem as follows: the Augustinian hypothesis holds that Matthew's gospel was the first, that Mark used Matthew, and that Luke was last using both of the former. The Griesbach hypothesis puts Matthew first; Luke was second and made use of the former, whilst Mark was last, drawing on the other two. However, the Oxford hypothesis remains the most popular, and it places Mark first, Matthew second making use of the former as well as a postulated document now lost, designated "Q", and Luke last, drawing on both Mark and Q. There is also the Farrer hypothesis that rejects Q and places the three synoptics in the order Mark–Matthew–Luke. In defense of Markan priority, McKnight argues that Mark is the shortest and most primitive account, and that it has been expanded by the other two writers. He notes that 90 percent of the Mark is contained in Matthew, and 53 percent in Luke, but believes that the latter two are independent although they used the common source of "Q" in addition to Mark, plus material of their own.

The fourth Gospel, that of John, was probably the last to be written, being completed in its present form in the late eighties or early nineties AD, or even a little later. The author is anonymous, and is only referred to as "the disciple whom Jesus loved . . . who testifies to these things and wrote them down" (John 21: 20 and 24). He is held by many to be the apostle John, son of Zebedee and brother of James, called by Jesus (Mark 1:19) and thus an eyewitness of the Messiah's life and teaching. In fact Donald Guthrie[23] notes that the statement: "We have seen his glory" (John 1:14) implies that he was among the witnesses to Jesus' works. John was a

---

22. McKnight, *Interpreting the Synoptic Gospels*, 35–40.

23. Guthrie, *New Testament Introduction*, 242–44.

close associate of Peter, and he was also close to Jesus in the upper room, which adds to his credibility as the one whom Jesus loved. John Marsh[24] points out that it is clear that the fourth gospel corrects some of the statements found in the synoptics, and that this would have been difficult for anyone who was not an apostle.

However, if the suggested date is correct, John the apostle would have been a very old man by the time he wrote his book. Alternative theories of authorship have been suggested, even though they usually retain links to the apostle as witness. One example is "John the elder", who uses this designation at the start of both the second and third letters of John, and another is John Mark mentioned in Acts 12:25,[25] whilst some prefer to refer to a Johannine tradition and a possible joint authorship. Marsh also mentions that nowhere in the gospel is John mentioned by name, and that chapter 21, which contains the reference to the disciple whom Jesus loved, is an appendix added to a book already completed, which otherwise appears to end naturally at the close of chapter 20. The question is, therefore: was this appendix added by John or by someone else, for example an editor, and does the reference to the enigmatic loved disciple who wrote the text refer to the whole gospel?

This book differs from the Synoptic Gospels, with very few overlaps with them, and it mentions neither the birth of Jesus nor the twelve disciples.[26] Whereas the synoptics concentrate on the Galilean ministry, the entire second half of John deals with just the last few days of Jesus' life and resurrection. As Donald Guthrie[27] observes, John himself makes the purpose of his book clear: "But these are written that you may believe that Jesus is the Messiah." (20:31). In other words, it was intended as an evangelistic instrument to produce faith in Jesus as Christ and Son of God. No intended audience is mentioned, but the book may have been written for the author's colleagues in Asia Minor where he worked after Jesus' death, or simply for a general readership.

24. Marsh, *Saint John*, 21–29.
25. Ibid.,
26. Butler, "John, Gospel of," 362–64.
27. Guthrie, *New Testament Introduction*, 242–44.

The book of Revelation is the last one in the Bible and it may also have been the last to have been written. Although some scholars think it may have been penned before the fall of Jerusalem in 70 AD, the majority prefer to date it around 90–95 AD as the message makes the most sense if this were the case.[28] Several verses in the book, including verse one, names the writer as "John", which would suggest the apostle John, son of Zebedee, who would have had first hand knowledge of Jesus.[29] However, the same considerations apply as were discussed in relation to the fourth gospel, not the least being that John the apostle would have been a very old man when he wrote this book, especially with a date as late as 95 AD. Verse nine states that John, the author, was in exile on the island of Patmos at that time, being banished there because of his faith and his preaching about Jesus; banishment was a lesser punishment than some other early Christians had received. Assuming the suggested date range is correct, the region remained under Roman rule at that time, and the emperor was Domitian, who reined from 81 to 96 AD.

John would have lived through a series of momentous events that occurred under a succession of evil local and national rulers. These included the crucifixion of his teacher, the robbing and subsequent destruction of the Jerusalem temple, civil war between Jews and Gentiles, infighting led by the Zealots, the suicides at Masada, and the end of Jewish authority.[30] Jerusalem lay mostly in shambles, and many Christians had fled to Asia Minor and had established churches there, including the seven to which John specifically addresses his message. The challenges being faced by the named churches at that time included being surrounded by false teachers, paganism, and persecution. In addition, they were being denied access to trade guilds (in Smyrna), they were in conflict with the local synagogue (in Philadelphia), and they had to

---

28. Couch, "Inerrancy: The book of Revelation," 206–16.

29. Keener, *Revelation*.

30. Schurer, *The History of the Jewish People*.

contend with those at Laodicea being so self-sufficient that Jesus was being shut out.[31]

Revelation, which contains over 350 Old Testament quotations and allusions, brings a message of comfort for the early church, and a hope for the future, plus an assurance that God will ultimately bring victory.[32] Trent Butler[33] notes that John calls for faithfulness and steadfast allegiance in the face of suffering, and that those who hold the Lord's prophecy will receive blessings. The persecuted churches must remain vigilant and resist compromise; even martyrdom is better than submission.[34] The book concludes with a graphic and symbolic description of the events of the end of time, the second coming of Jesus, victory for the redeemed, and what the New Jerusalem will be like.[35]

31. Keener, *Revelation*.

32. McCartney and Clayton, *Let the Reader Understand*.

33. Butler, "Revelation." 531–34.

34. Keener, *Revelation*."

35. Couch, "Inerrancy: Book of Revelation," 206–16.

CHAPTER 4

THE EPISTLES AS EVIDENCE

FIVE OF PAUL'S EPISTLES provide pertinent references on end of life issues and despair. F. F. Bruce[1] relates that Paul was born during the first decade of the first century AD, in the city of Tarsus in Cilicia. He was an observant Jew, and his family could trace their origins to the tribe of Benjamin. Paul also had the rare privilege of Roman citizenship, inherited at birth, and was able to make use of this during his career. He received his education in Jerusalem, and excelled in the study and practice of Judaism. Paul was an active persecutor of the church until, on his way to Damascus with a commission to round up Christians who had sought refuge there, he had his famous conversion experience (see Acts 9:1–6). He had seen and heard Jesus, and the Law that had governed Paul's life up to then had been displaced. From then on he followed his call to evangelize and, in his extensive travels to establish the Christian church, he met and journeyed with others who are named in the Bible, including Peter, James and Barnabas. He is believed to have been beheaded in Rome around the year 65 AD.

Thirteen of Paul's letters survive, and they are generally thought to comprise the earliest authenticated Christian texts, being gathered together perhaps as early as 85 AD. There is lack of complete agreement on their precise dates and locations. Suggested dates for what may be the earliest letters range from 49–57 AD for Galatians, 50–51 AD for 1 Thessalonians, and 52–61 AD

---

1. Bruce, "Paul in Acts and Letters," 679–92.

for Colossians. With regard to those epistles used in the present enquiry, Paul's letter to the Romans could have been written sometime between 55 and 59 AD, whilst he was in Corinth. Rome was the first city in the Western Mediteranian to embrace Christianity, and it may have been introduced there by Jewish Christians returning from Palestine.[2] Paul was aware that the church at Rome did not have an apostolic founder, and that there was friction between the resident Gentile Christians and the Jews returning after having been banished in 49 AD by Claudius for being disruptive. Douglas Moo[3] suggests that Paul wrote this letter both to address such issues, and to plan his first visit to there.

Paul established the church in Corinth in 51–52 AD, and 1 Corinthians was probably written whilst he was in Ephesus around 53–56 AD. He wrote to address the divisiveness about which he had heard, and specifically that some people were aligning themselves to different apostles, including himself, Apollos and Cephas rather than to Christ.[4] Paul tries to counter this by emphasizing that they were all servants of Jesus and should be supporting each other, not competing (1 Cor 3:5–9). The second letter to the Corinthians was probably written about a year after the first, and it expresses relief that Titus had brought him good news that the animosity that was previously directed at Paul in Corinth had now subsided.[5] He also comments about his proposed return visit there, and his plans for a collection for the needy Christians in Judea.

The Epistle to the Ephesians, along with that to the Philippians, are among the four believed to have been written by Paul during his first imprisonment in Rome around 61–63 AD, but some deny Pauline authorship and also allocate a later date.[6] Guthrie adds that the content of the letter is more reflective here than in any other of Paul's letters, and that the intention may have been to provide a summary of his doctrine. Additionally, despite the ad-

2. Russell, "Insights from Postmodernism's Emphasis," 511–25.

3. Moo, *Encountering the Book of Romans*.

4. Erickson, *Christian Theology*, 1011–18.

5. Guthrie, *New Testament Introduction*, 438–39.

6. Ibid., 515–16.

dressee being stated in the first verse as the Ephesians ("To God's holy people in Ephesus", although this is not included in all the early manuscripts), it may have been intended as a circular-letter to house churches in that city, and even more widely.[7] This notion is bolstered by the lack of reference to a specific situation or real problems, as it is directed in a more pastoral way to the general needs and conduct of a developing Christian community.

The date of the last Pauline epistle that was consulted, that to the Philippians, depends on where the author was at the time he wrote it. If, as mentioned above in conjunction with Ephesians, this is one of the letters he wrote whilst imprisoned in Rome, then it would likewise date from 61 to 63 AD. Paul was still a prisoner, as evidence by statements such as ". . . it has become clear throughout the whole palace guard that I am in chains for Christ" (Phil 1:13). Alternative suggestions of Paul's whereabouts are Caesarea, inter alia because the "palace" could have been Herod's in that city, and Ephesus, partly because it is closer to Philippi than is Rome for travel and communication.[8]

Gerald Hawthorne[9] adds Corinth as a possible origin, which was even closer to Philippi than was Ephesus. If Corinth is the location, then he suggests the early date of about 50 AD, but 54–57 AD if Ephesus, and 58–60 AD if Caesarea. Hawthorne also states that the church in Philippi in Macedonia was the first that Paul founded in Europe. This was during his second missionary journey, which took place from 49 to 52 AD.[10] The letter contains advice on how Christians should live in this world, in harmony, unafraid of opponents, and being willing to suffer for their gospel. It can be seen from this and the other Pauline epistles that a recurring theme is on how to cope with adversity, even in the face of personal hardships. This will no doubt have a bearing on why selected passages from these books have been nominated as relevant

---

7. Arnold, "Ephesians," 238–53.

8. Guthrie, *New Testament Introduction*, 526–36.

9. Hawthorne, "Philippians," 707–13.

10. Butler, "Paul"; "Philippians," 477; 487.

to end of life issues and situations of despair, as will be discussed in later chapters.

Although the letter to the Hebrews bears some resemblance to Paul's thoughts and style, the writer is unknown. It was only adopted into the canon somewhat later than were most of the other books, on the supposition of a Pauline link.[11] Other suggested authors have included Luke, Timothy, Silvanus, Philip, Priscilla, Philo, Jude, and Mary.[12] [13] [14] However, the writer was likely to have been a second-generation Christian, probably Jewish and from Alexandria, a teacher, and one well-versed in Old Testament scripture.[15] Paul Ellingworth[16] notes that there are 35 direct Old Testament quotes in Hebrews, and the Good News Bible cross-references 131 passages, whilst George Guthrie[17] lists 421 Old Testament entries for Hebrews. Martin Luther's suggestion of Apollos, an eloquent preacher and acquaintance of Paul, has received wide support,[18] but Daniel Wallace[19] favors a joint authorship of Apollos and the Levite Barnabas.

The letter was probably written around 65 AD, after Paul's death,[20] as hinted at in 13:7 ("remember your former leaders . . . how they lived and died" GNB). Timothy was still alive (13:23), and there was no suggestion that the fall of Jerusalem (70 AD) had yet taken place.[21] The target readership may have been a local community of second-generation Jewish-Christians, possibly a house group who had, or were experiencing, some level of challenge to

---

11. Neil, *Epistle to the Hebrews*.

12. Guthrie, *New Testament Introduction*.

13. Parsons, "Son and High Priest," 195–216.

14. Ellingworth, *Epistle to the Hebrews*.

15. Evans, *Communicator's commentary: Hebrews*.

16. Ibid.

17. Guthrie, "Hebrews," 919–95.

18. Neil, *Epistle to the Hebrews*.

19. Wallace, *Hebrews: Introduction*.

20. Guthrie, New *Testament Introduction*.

21. Peterson, "Hebrews," 1321–53.

their faith prior to this date (10:32 "Remember these early days . . . when you endured in a great conflict full of suffering").

The animosity toward Christians in Rome, and the anticipation of the Neronic persecution to come, would have generated a troublesome time for Christians, and a temptation to revert to the Jewish faith that would have afforded them some protection.[22] The writer tries to encourage the readers to maintain their faith, and that Jesus, as High Priest, will provide salvation from sin, fear and death. Whilst Rome is a favored destination, Alexandria and Jerusalem have also been mooted, but Daniel Wallace[23] suggests that it is the Lycos Valley in Asia Minor (now Turkey), whilst Mikeal Parsons[24] opines that the intended readers comprised a group in Qumran that held many Christian beliefs.

Two further epistles yielded potentially useful advice for this investigation. The first letter from Peter is attributed by most scholars to the apostle of that name. According to Trent Butler,[25] this was written in Rome about 62–64 AD, during the time of Nero's persecution of believers, and was intended for converted Jews and Gentiles. The geographical destination is stated in the first verse, where several nations within Asia Minor are cited including Pontus, Galatia and Cappadocia. David Wheaton[26] states that a messenger would have taken the letter to the main churches there, where it would be copied for the smaller centers of Christian witness. He adds that Peter anticipates the risk of persecution faced by the Christians, encourages them to remain steadfast during these difficult times, and be confident of God's ultimate deliverance through the suffering of Jesus Christ and the presence of the Holy Spirit. Thus, again, the message is to persevere in the face of adversity.

Finally, there is the first letter of John, traditionally agreed to have been written by the apostle of that name, and it is similar

---

22. Neil, *Epistle to the Hebrews.*

23. Wallace, *Hebrews: Introduction.*

24. Parsons, "Son and high priest," 195–216.

25. Butler, "Peter, First Letter," 484–85.

26. Wheaton, "1 Peter," 1369–85.

in style to John's gospel.[27] Although Donald Guthrie[28] suggests the date of authorship as 90–95 AD, being written slightly after the gospel, this raises the same potential problem of the great age that the apostle John would have been at the time of writing. To surmount this difficulty, some prefer to refer to a Johannine tradition or school, accepting that these various writings all reflect the thoughts of the apostle even if he did not write them (see also discussion in chapter 3). Guthrie suggests that this letter was written to groups of people in one or more Asiatic communities who were threatened by the infiltration of a form of false teaching that was an early type of Gnosticism. In particular, as Leon Morris notes, the people were denying the incarnation, which would be to take the heart out of Christianity. But the message is also a positive one, in that John wrote to take away anxiety, to confirm that Jesus Christ was a real human being, and to emphasize that all who believe must love one another.

27. Morris, "1 John," 1397–1409.

28. Guthrie, *New Testament Introduction*, 883–84.

CHAPTER 5

THE PROBLEMS OF BIBLICAL INTERPRETATION

ASK ANYONE FOR A Bible quotation that deals with the ethics of ending a life, and the chances are that the person will offer the traditional King James' Version of Exodus 20:13 "Thou shalt not kill". Does this mean that the quest to seek guidance on this issue is at an end, with an emphatic condemnation of euthanasia? Far from it, because this raises another question, namely, is it possible to establish the intended meaning of a text with any degree of accuracy, after the passage of two thousand years in the case of the New Testament, and much longer in the case of the Old, and in a different cultural, political and geographical situation (the *Sitz im Leben*) to that pertaining when the words were recorded?

In other words, before we can safely use the texts for guidance today, it is first necessary to try and establish what they conveyed at the time they were written. The process of trying to interpret the original meaning of scripture in an unbiased a way as possible is "exegesis", but the risk is that it may end up as "eisegesis"— the imposing of one's own thoughts and fancies on the meaning of a text. Grant Osborne[1] calls the whole process the "hermeneutical spiral" meaning that, through repeated processes of interpretation, contemplation and re-interpretation, we spiral in ever closer to the true meaning of the passage, although this still remains open-ended for yet further exegesis.

1. Osborne, *Hermeneutical Spiral,* 6.

The process of exegesis, or criticism as it is sometimes called, can take various forms, several of which can be run sequentially if required. Drawing inter alia on the discussion by Millard Erickson,[2] some of these can be summarized as follows. Firstly, textural criticism involves comparing various existing biblical manuscripts of the same narrative, to see if there are any significant differences between them. If there are, then the most likely original wording should be deduced, if this is possible. Literary-source criticism is the process of trying to identify the literary origins upon which a biblical book is based, whereas form criticism involves efforts to determine the oral tradition behind the written sources. It is surmised that some of the authors, writing several decades after the actual events as they did, may have tried to fit some vague stories or sayings of Jesus together in a more coherent form. Apart from the risk of losing the original context, the writers would have been prone to influence by a cultural milieu that had changed in the meantime, for example by becoming more Greek and less Jewish.

Redaction criticism involves an attempt to determine how the activities and perspectives of an author may have influenced his interpretation of the events on which he wrote. This is especially useful when more than one person has written about the same topic, for example in the Synoptic Gospels where there are sometimes parallel accounts of the same event. An author's view will have been influenced by such factors as his own presuppositions, whether he came from a Jewish or Greek background, the context of Jesus' pronouncements and actions, and the situation faced by the church at the time he eventually committed his account to paper. Finally, historical criticism draws on these and other types of analysis, plus it takes account of archaeological discoveries and historical evidence from other sources, in an attempt to determine the truth of what occurred historically.

Whilst a whole book would be necessary to discuss in detail all the techniques that scholars use to try and arrive at an accurate understanding of the biblical texts, the above review should suffice

2. Erickson, *Christian Theology*, 81–102.

to assure the reader that appropriate methodologies are employed, and that prodigious efforts are made to try and arrive at the truth. Even when one is confident that a sound rendition of the original event has been achieved, there is at least one other major consideration to take into account. Throughout history scholars have seesawed between a largely allegorical interpretation of the Scriptures, as practiced for example by the Alexandrian patristic school, and a more plain and literal understanding, as favored by the school at Antioch.[3] A more detailed look at these two influential schools may help to explain why there is still sometimes a lack of consensus between scholars on just what a particular text means.

Alexandria was founded by Alexander the Great, and was the capital of Egypt from 330 BC. It was also the most important centre of Judaism outside Jerusalem.[4] In the second century BC, 70 Jewish scholars undertook the translation of the Hebrew Scriptures into Greek and, by the beginning of the third century AD, this centre was regarded as the intellectual capital of the Roman Empire. Alexandria took the lead in biblical interpretation, typically drawing on the methodology of an earlier Jewish scholar, Philo (20 BC–50 AD), who believed that scripture had both a "body" (literal meaning) and a "soul" (spiritual meaning).[5] The literal sense should be denied if, for example, it implied something unworthy of God or contained inconsistencies or impossibilities.[6]

Philo had learned to divide the non-literal, or allegorical, meaning into the physical and the ethical, corresponding to the nature of God and the moral duties of man.[7] He, along with the later Alexandrians, were inspired both by the writings of Plato, who held that the world around us is a shadowy picture of true reality and it is this that we perceive rather than the actual, and by the Stoics who believed that messages encoded in the

---

3. Bray, *Biblical Interpretation*, 77–89.

4. Butler, "Alexandria," 17.

5. Klein et al., *Introduction to Biblical Interpretation*..

6. Young, "Alexandrian Interpretation," 10–12.

7. Grant and Tracy, *Short History*.

scriptures were coherent, rational and accessible through non-literal interpretation.[8]

Clement (C150–215 AD) introduced Philonic exegesis into the church, in order to base his Christian faith on a secure scientific foundation.[9] He became leader of the Alexandrian school in 190 AD,[10] and believed that the truth of scripture comes through a veil, and needs interpretation—the key is Jesus Christ.[11] Clement believed that the voice of God speaks through all the biblical texts, and that the writers became the interpreters of that divine voice. It is therefore necessary to look beyond the words to hear the voice behind the literal text. What is written in the New Testament may appear in symbolic language in the Old Testament, and thus it needs to be read allegorically.[12]

Clement was the first Christian to justify and explain the meaning of the allegorical method, even though he was not very systematic and had the tendency to use scripture to illustrate his already formed thought.[13] Dan McCartney and Charles Clayton[14] note that he believed that the true meaning of scripture is hidden from the "common man" by allegories, which only the "higher" Christian could interpret. His three principles of interpretation were firstly that nothing is literally true that is unworthy of God, secondly that no interpretation is accepted that contradicts the Bible as a whole and, thirdly, that the literal meaning is meant to excite interest in understanding the deeper meaning. Thus, for Clement, the literal meaning was just the starting point.[15]

Origen (C184–253 AD) was more systematic and scholarly than was Clement. He acknowledged the literal meaning of scripture, but maintained that its importance lay in the moral and

8. Stallard, "Literal Interpretation," 14–55.

9. Bray, *Biblical Interpretation*.

10. Dockery, "History of Pre-critical Biblical Interpretation," 1–30.

11. Young, "Alexandrian Interpretation, 10–12.

12. Wylie, "Clement of Alexandria," 35–39.

13. Grant and Tracy, *Short History*.

14. McCartney and Clayton, *Let the Rader Understand*.

15. Dockery, "History of Pre-critical Biblical Interpretation," 1–30.

spiritual meaning. His aim was to reach knowledge of the transcendent God, for which an allegorical interpretation was needed.[16] Origen thought that the purpose of scripture lay in the resolution of "intellectual truths" rather than the God of history: the fulfillment of prophecy is the proof of inspiration.[17] As Robertson McQuilkin[18] notes, Origen held that everything written in the Bible had a figurative meaning. He fought against the Gnostic attack on the church's belief that Jesus' father was the same as the creator God of the Old Testament, and sought to do so rationally and to preserve the whole biblical canon.[19] Origen based his exegesis on the belief that scripture had three different meanings: the literal, moral, and allegorical, corresponding to a threefold division of humankind: the moral, emotional (Psychical), and spiritual (intellectual).[20]

Turning now to the school of Antioch, this town was sited in Syria, some 20 miles inland, and was the third largest city of the Roman Empire, after Rome itself and Alexandria. It was founded around 300 BC by Seleceus Nicator.[21] Acts 11:19 states that Jewish believers settled there to escape persecution, and it is where they were first called Christians; John Polhill[22] explains that these people would be Hellenist Jews. Charles Kannengiesser[23] adds that the priest Lucian (C240–312 AD) is considered to be the founder of the exegetical tradition of Antioch, although R. M. Grant and D. Tracy[24] suggest that the earliest example of Antiochene exegesis was an interpretation of Genesis by Theophilus (C120–183 AD), but that this was largely derived from Jewish teachers. Diodore of Tarsus (d. C394 AD) was a renowned scholar of Antioch; he

16. Young, "Alexandrian Interpretation," 10–12.

17. Grant and Tracy, *Short History*.

18. McQuilkin, *Understanding and Applying the Bible*.

19. Nassif, "Origin," 52–60.

20. Dockery, "History of Pre-critical Biblical Interpretation," 1–30.

21. Butler, "Antioch," 30.

22. Polhill, "Antioch's Contribution," 3–19.

23. Kannengiesser, "Antiochene and Syrian Traditions," 1–16.

24. Grant and Tracy, *Short History*.

rejected the allegorization practiced at Alexandria and stuck to the historical and grammatical method of exegesis.

One of the most significant practitioners of the Antiochene School was Theodore of Mopsuestia (C350–428 AD), who criticized Alexandrian allegorical methodology because it can lead to impiety, blasphemy and falsehood.[25] He advocated the practice of plain meaning, declaring that no text can imitate something other than what it openly says, although it may be by figure of speech.[26] Thus, Theodore believed that very few Old Testament passages refer to Jesus Christ, but that they were confined to the Mosaic dispensation. He developed the principle that, unless the New Testament actually cites an Old Testament text, it is not messianic: an allusion is not sufficient evidence, and the reference might only be illustrative.[27] Theodore regarded references to the Old Testament in the New as being typology, in that certain events in the Old prefigured some in the New or, in other words, observing a pattern set up earlier that a person or event later explains.[28]

Gerald Bray[29] states that Theodore wrote many commentaries, followed a scientific approach, and was the first scholar to make extensive use of literary criticism. David Dockery,[30] however, suggests that Theodore's exegesis was more Jewish than was the case with some of his contemporaries, and that he rejected interpretations that denied historical reality. Theodore attempted a unified theological exposition, and viewed the Bible as a record of historical development of the divine redemptive plan.

A contemporary, and indeed friend of Theodore, was John Chrysostom (C347–407 AD), a priest at Antioch. He regarded the historical meaning of a text as authoritative, and that the final form

25. Ibid.
26. Norris, "Antiochene Interpretation, "29–32.
27. McCartney and Clayton, *Let the Reader Understand.*
28. McDonald, *Historical Handbook*, 65–69.
29. Bray, *Biblical Interpretation.*
30. Dockery, "History of Pre-critical Biblical Interpretation," 1–30.

is found in the typological meaning.[31] Margaret Mitchell[32] notes that Chrysostom's exegesis was logical, literal, sober, restrained, commonsensical, grammatical, detailed, and historical, which was typically Antiochene. Chrysostom believed that God had to speak to humans in their language, with all its limitations, and his emphasis was on the human author, and that no word should be neglected. He did not, however, ignore the spiritual sense of the text but believed it was literally expressed and could be applied to the immediate needs of his flock.[33] Whereas the Alexandrian School based its exegesis on Plato's rather "other-worldly" view, Chrysostom and the other Antiochenes preferred to follow the more down-to-earth philosophy of Aristotle.[34]

Does what has been written so far imply that there were two mutually exclusive schools of exegesis, Alexandria and Antioch, during the time of the Church Fathers? Donald Fairbairn[35] states that the Antiochenes, with their literalism, are often seen as the "good guys", and the Alexandrians with their allegorization being the "bad guys". In reality, those from Antioch sometimes allegorized passages that their colleagues from Alexandria took literally. To cite just one example, Theodore of Antioch interprets "flesh" in John 1:14 as signifying Jesus, whilst Clement of Alexandria believed that the literal sense must first be observed and that, rather than resorting to boundless allegorization, the rule of faith provided a guide to interpretation.

In similar vein, whilst Origen might be regarded as an ardent allegorist, he nevertheless affirmed the literal inspiration of every word of the scriptures, even though this might not be the primary sense. He held that the literal meaning may attract believers initially by its teachings on morals and behavior but, as people develop, they come to understand the deeper truths.[36] As R. A.

---

31. Grant and Tracy, *Short History*.

32. Mitchell, "Chrysostom, John," 28–34.

33. Bray, *Biblical Interpretation*.

34. Dockery, History of Pre-critical Biblical Interpretation," 1–30.

35. Fairburn, "Historical and Theological Studies," 1–30.

36. Dockery, "History of Pre-critical Interpretation," 1–30.

Norris[37] observes, a problem is that some passages just cannot be literal, for example the statement "God is my rock" (2 Sam 22:3), to which may be added "God is light" (I John 1:5). They add that those who demand dogmatic acceptance of a text are unaware of the complexities, and that they may manipulate the letter of the scripture in the interests of consistency.

Thus it may be concluded that the two patristic schools, whilst being conveniently associated with contrasting exegetical method-ology, were not really polar opposites. Mike Stallard[38] comments that it is not possible to see a complete contrast between Alexandria and Antioch: there was interest in literal interpretation at times in the former, whilst typological interpretations were sometimes applied by the latter. There was thus an overlap of approach that did not blur definite tendencies. This would concur with the view of Donald Fairburn[39] that, whilst Origen was the most extreme of the Alexandrian allegorists, and Theodore of Antioch the most opposed to this, by the time of Theodoret of Cyrus (393–457 AD), who was born in Antioch, there was no rigid distinction between the two schools but rather a synthesis. What led to apparent dif-ferences was theology, with the Antiochenes contrasting with the Alexandrians in emphasizing the full humanity of Jesus.[40] [41]

The above somewhat lengthy discussion on biblical interpre-tation is intended to help the reader understand the challenges associated with simply quoting a text from the Bible, and then accepting it at face value as a guide to moral behavior. In view of the difficulty of deducing the true meaning of what was written at the time it was penned, and what it means for us today, it is not surprising that using biblical texts to support or condemn ethical decisions can result in more disagreement than consensus.

37. Norris, "Antiochene Interpretation," 29–32.
38. Stallard, "Literal Interpretation," 14–55.
39. Fairburn, "Historical and Theological Studies," 1–30.
40. Ibid.
41. Polhill, "Antioch's Contribution to Christianity," 3–19.

CHAPTER 6

WHAT'S THE POINT: DO WE HAVE FREE WILL?

BEFORE EMBARKING ON A detailed examination of biblical texts that might inform on the ethics of assisted dying and despair, there is a further very relevant point that needs to be considered. This concerns whether or not we actually have freedom in all that we do, or whether everything is predestined and out of our control. There would seem little to be gained by agonizing over ethical decisions, and diligently seeking guidance from the scriptures or any other source, if whatever happens, and whatever we may decide, is predestined anyway.

In reality, just how free are we, assuming that we are not in prison or otherwise constrained against our will? The discussion that follows draws on notes taken at a lecture given by Rev. Chris Lazenby.[1] It is clear that we cannot just behave in any way we wish regardless of any consequences, as we are restricted by many forces. In the first instance, physical restraint or our own lack of ability might prevent us from acting on an impulse. Even when we are physically able to do so, we would usually resist committing acts that are against the law. Whilst hopefully our individual sense of fairness, or even fear of reprisal, will prevent us from doing things that hurt or upset others, laws are there to prevent people from exercising their own freedom at the expense of the freedom, welfare or safety of their fellow human beings. Thus, if only be-

1. Lazenby, "Do Christians Exercise Free Will?"

cause of such practical constraints, we are on weak ground if we claim that we are, in reality, free to behave as we wish, and this may also apply to ethical decisions.

It also remains a matter of opinion, or faith, whether or not God will ultimately embrace into his divine plan the non-Christian and also the sinner. For the already committed Christian, however, the situation might be different. Several passages in the Bible point to God knowing our thoughts and knowing the future, for example "You know when I sit and when I rise; you perceive my thoughts from afar" (Psalm 139: 2) and, in referring to Israel being adopted as the chosen race, Isaiah 44:8 states: "Did I not proclaim this and foretell it long ago?"

Indeed, some believe that God makes us behave in certain ways whether we like it or not, such as: "I have raised you up for this very purpose" (Ex 9:16) and, with regard to Joshua's battles to gain possession of the Promised Lands: "for it was the Lord himself who hardened their (i.e. the kings') hearts to wage war against Israel" (Josh 11:20). However, this does not mean that we can in theory do anything that God may require, because we have human limitations and God has to work with these.

These texts seem to point in the direction of us not having free will, as does Genesis 50:20 with reference to Joseph being ill-treated by his brothers: "You intended to harm me, but God intended it for good to accomplish what is now being done." In the New Testament Jesus is quoted as saying: "All these things have been committed to me by my father" (Matt 11:27), and in John 6:37 "All those the father gives me will come to me" adding later "You did not choose me, but I chose you" (18:16). Paul's statement in Ephesians 1:4–5 appears to leave little room for doubt that all that happens is by God's hand: "For he chose us in him before the creation of the world . . . he predestined us for adoption to sonship through Jesus Christ, in accordance with his pleasure and will."

Should the discussion on free-will end here, or are there passages that give some support for our freedom? Starting again with Genesis, it seems clear that Adam and Eve had a choice in whether or not to eat the forbidden fruit. God says: "You are free to eat from any tree in the garden; but you must not eat from the tree of knowledge of good and evil" (2:19–17). However, Eve exercises her freedom and ignores God's command. Joshua writes that he said to the assembled tribes of Israel: "But if serving the Lord seems undesirable to you, then choose for yourselves this day whom you will serve" (24:15). In the New Testament Peter writes: "For you have spent enough time in the past doing what pagans choose to do" (1 Pet 4:3), and Paul asks when contemplating his future life: "Yet what shall I choose? I do not know!" (Philippians 1:22).

Thus, once again, there are texts that appear to provide confirmation for each of the alternative views, and this is the inevitable consequence of proof-texting to seek support for a pre-determined opinion. If one is able to commence a biblical search from a standpoint devoid of any presuppositions, simply citing passages that appear relevant for the topic in question is likely to prove inconclusive. In order to try and make progress, it is necessary to follow a more detailed interpretation—or exegesis—of each text, taking account of the reliability of the account, the situation pertaining at the time the words were written, and the original meaning that was intended by the author. Even this may lead to a lack of consensus, because some will favor a literal interpretation whilst others will see the writing as allegorical, as was discussed in chapter 5.

Whilst it may seem that there is a stalemate with regard to freedom versus determinism per se, the situation for the committed Christian is clearer. John 8:31–36 reports Jesus as saying: "you will know the truth, and the truth will set you free . . . everyone who sins is a slave to sin . . . if the son sets you free, you will be free indeed." Thus, Christians are freed from the law of sin and are free to do God's will; what *they* would like to do is what *God* would like them to do. Despite this, human weaknesses can prevent a person doing God's will, as Paul so plaintively laments in a remarkable admission, commencing Romans 7:14. He states: "I do not understand what I do. For what I want to do I do not do, but what I hate I do" (v. 15). "For I do not do the good I want to do, but the evil I do not want to do—this I keep doing" (v. 19). "What a wretched man I am! (v. 24).

If Paul himself struggles to do what is right, then there would seem to be little hope for lesser mortals. We shall ourselves no doubt struggle when faced with ethical decisions, and try to find guidance from all available sources, including the scriptures. Whilst the discussion contained in the chapters still to come may help, Paul himself offers some advice: "Do not conform to the pattern of this world, but be transformed by the renewing of your mind. Then you will be able to test and approve what God's will is—his good, pleasing and perfect will." (Rom 12:2).

CHAPTER 7

UNIVERSALISM

THE QUESTION OF WHETHER or not we are free to take decisions, including ethical ones, as discussed in chapter 6, can be extended into an even more fundamental concern. This is: do the actions that we take in this life ultimately affect our standing with God or, as some put it, whether or not we shall achieve salvation and go to heaven? Indeed this is a major consideration, especially for Christians, and it is part of the wider issue of "inclusivism" —the view that God's salvation is offered to all who respond appropriately, versus "particularism"—the belief that God predestines some for salvation but passes over others. If Paul is correct, referring to what God said to Moses, nothing we can do will influence this: "I will have mercy on whom I have mercy . . . it does not, therefore, depend on human desire or effort" (Rom 9: 15–16).

"Universalism" extends inclusivism to the level where it is believed that we shall all ultimately be saved, whether we respond positively to God or not. Whilst those who subscribe to inclusivism might believe that the decisions they make in this life, whether ethical ones or otherwise, could influence their standing with God and ultimate salvation, Universalists would likely not worry so much about such consequences. For the sake of completion, mention can be made of "religious exclusivism", the followers of which maintain that there is no salvation for those who do not subscribe to Christianity, in contrast to "religious inclusivism" that upholds the view that God is present in all religions.[1]

Many biblical texts seem to imply that all shall be saved, come what may. In the Old Testament, Trent Butler[2] notes especially Isaiah 25:6–8: "The Lord Almighty will prepare a feast for all peoples . . . (he) will destroy the shroud that enfolds all peoples . . . will swallow up death for ever." Although the mention of "all peoples" seems unambiguous, the message at that time was addressed to the Israelites and may have excluded those who were not of the chosen race, as later in the same chapter the Moabites are said to be "brought down to the ground, to the very dust" (v. 12).

Pertinent New Testament texts that have been cited in support of Universalism, inter alia by Millard Erickson[3] include Jesus saying: "And I, when I am lifted up from the earth, will draw all people to myself" (John 12:32). Examples of statements by others are: "God does not show favoritism" (Acts 10:34); "Life for all people" (Rom 5:18); "God, who is the savior of all people" (1 Tim 4:10); "he died for all" (2 Cor 5:15); and "The Lord . . . is patient with you, not wanting anyone to perish" (2 Pet 3:9).

However, such selective proof-texting out of context rarely yields unequivocal evidence, especially to the skeptic. Whilst most of these examples are utterances of admittedly pious followers of Jesus, only the John reference is given the added authority of being a direct saying of the Christ. Although these passages may suggest the potential for universal salvation, the more complete texts often indicate that this is conditional. For example, the Acts 10 statement mentioned above continues ". . . but (God) accepts . . . the one who fears him and does what is right", whilst the 1 Timothy passage adds ". . . and especially of those who believe."

The earliest champion of Universalism was probably Origen the Alexandrian who, as discussed in chapter 5, favored allegorical interpretation in order to arrive at scripture's moral and spiritual

---

1. Geivett, "Misgivings" and "Openness," 26–37.
2. Butler, "Salvation," 550–51.
3. Erickson, "The Extent of Salvation," 1015–22.

meaning.[4] According to Millard Erickson,[5] Origen believed that the wicked would be only temporally separated from God, and that ultimately all things will be restored. This is the doctrine of *apokatastasis*: the Greek term for restoration of a thing to its former state.[6] Origen's views were condemned by the Synod of Constantinople in 543 AD, and also by Augustine who said that it was wrong to deny hell.[7]

Support for Universalism was spasmodic at best over the centuries but, in more modern times, Schleiermacher (1768–1834) thought that treating Old Testament (Jewish) scripture as an authoritative source for Christian doctrine was wrong.[8] He also argued against the prevailing view of hell, believing that the blessed redeemed would be marred by their sympathy for the damned, and that all are elected to salvation in Christ.[9] Bauckham also commented that John Hick (1922–2012) said it would deny God's omnipotent love if there was no ultimate universal salvation. However, Paul Helm[10] opined that Hick's view that the threats of punishment mentioned in the Bible were merely warnings and challenges was wrong: if people ignore the threat, then Jesus can not ignore the punishment.

By contrast, texts that imply salvation only for the good, and eternal punishment or annihilation for the bad, are at least as numerous as are those supporting Universalism. In the Old Testament, with reference to the Israelites, it is written "only a remnant will return. Destruction has been decreed" (Isaiah, 10:22). This was later cited by Paul as "only a remnant will be saved. For the Lord will carry out his sentence" (Rom 10:27–28).

Examples in the New Testament this time do include direct quotes from Jesus himself. Among those cited by Millard

---

4. Young, "Alexandrian Interpretation," 10–12.

5. Erickson, "Extent of Salvation," 1015–22.

6. Friberg et al., *Analytical Lexicon of the Greek New Testament*, 68.

7. Beougher, "Are all Doomed to be Saved?" 6–24.

8. DeVries, "Schleiermacher," 350–55.

9. Bauckham, "Universalism," 47–54.

10. Helm, "Universalism," 35–43.

Erickson[11] and others are: "those who have done what is good will rise to live, and those who have done what is evil will rise to be condemned" (John 5:29); and "broad is the gate that leads to destruction, and many enter through it" (Matt 7:13). In Hebrews 9:27 we read: "people are destined to die once, and after that to face judgment".

On the basis of such proof-texts, whilst not ruling out the possibility that all *may* be saved, there is still evidence that salvation remains conditional. This is made specific in John 3:18 "Whoever does not believe (in Jesus) stands condemned." Richard Bauckham,[12] however, comments that the translation of the Greek *aiōnion* as "eternal" (or "for all time, forever")[13] is disputed. Thus, passages such as: "Depart from me, you who are cursed, into the eternal fire prepared for the devil and his angels" (Matt 25:41) may be misinterpreted.

Whilst the notion that all will be saved is something we would hope for and desire, some scholars doubt that the biblical evidence is sufficiently strong to support this. For example, and with specific relevance for ethical behavior, Timothy Beougher[14] notes that the Bible emphasizes the need to take decisions in this life, and be judged accordingly, whilst Richard Mayhue[15] concludes from his review of the evidence that the notion of eternal punishment for the wicked is correct, and that the alternative view of salvation for all is not supported by the scriptures.

Millard Erickson[16] adds to the discussion with his detailed comparison of texts that at least superficially seem to support either one view or the other, such as: "so in Christ all will be made alive" (1 Cor 15:22) in contrast to "whoever blasphemes . . . will never be forgiven" (Mark 3:29). He concludes, albeit without satisfaction that, whilst salvation is universally available, it is not in fact universal.

11. Erickson, "Final Judgment," 1203.

12. Bauckham, "Universalism," 47–54.

13. Friberg et al., *Analytical Lexicon of the Greek New Testament*, 39.

14. Beougher, "Are all Doomed to be Saved?" 6–24.

15. Mayhue, "Hell: Never, Forever," 129–45.

16. Erickson, "Extent of Salvation ," 1015–22.

Thus, not everyone will be saved. In the spirit of Rom 10:14–15 ("How beautiful are the feet of those who bring good news"), Erickson suggests that this should be a spur to evangelistic effort.

Is it possible to come to a conclusion on whether or not a failure to follow the ethical guidance offered by the Bible in matters such as assisted suicide will result in the wrath of God and punishment in the afterlife? If the answer is that we shall achieve salvation in any event, does this mean that we can then ignore what the Bible says on moral issues, and base our decisions on other criteria, including our own judgment? Just like other issues relating to biblical interpretation, some of which have been discussed already such as literalism versus allegory, it is inevitably going to be a matter of each individual weighing up the evidence and coupling this with the strength of his or her faith, in order to arrive at a conclusion that feels right. The following discussion on the argument presented thus far may be helpful.

Over 50 years ago, Harold Lindsell[17] observed that Universalism was enjoying a substantial resurgence, whilst more recently Timothy Beougher[18] stated that the notion that all will be saved may be popular in today's religious and cultural pluralism. However, relying on biblical proof-texts to "prove" universal salvation is dubious, as some of the previous evidence has indicated, so some scholars have turned to both rational and philosophical debate in an endeavor to offer a solution that satisfies the current climate. In an obvious reference to "religious inclucivism" (vide supra), Lindsell queried if the Christian faith really is the only vehicle of salvation, and whether or not God was also working through the adherents of other religions "whose lives seemed to manifest the note of the authentic".[19] He opined that there would be an incongruity between God's all-sovereign love and the exclusion of such people, as well as those who have not yet heard the Good News. If God is creator of all but cannot save all, then he is not sovereign.

17. Lindsell, "Universalism today," 209–17.
18. Beougher, "Are all Doomed to be Saved?" 6–24.
19. Lindsell, "Universalism today," 213.

Clark Pinnock also writes from an inclusivist position (see dialogue cited in Geivett, 1998)[20] and observes that there are hints of all-inclusive salvation in the Bible, for example in Acts 10:28 where Peter states: "God has shown me that I should not call anyone impure or unclean", adding in verse thirty-five: "God does not show favoritism but accepts from every nation." Pinnock states that there is support for the notion that God works through other religions to bring people to the faith, and he suggests that there could be "pre-messianic" believers who could convert if they heard the Good News. Passages that indicate that this is indeed the case include: "The true light that gives light to everyone was coming into the world" (John: 1:9); "God did this . . . he is not far from any one of us" (Acts 17:27); "To those who by persistence in doing good seek glory, honor and immortality, he will give eternal life" (Rom 2:7); and "This will take place on the day when God judges people's secrets through Jesus Christ, as my gospel declares" (Rom 2:16).

Some people have regarded the term Universalism as a multiple-variable concept. Robert Mackintosh[21] defined three of these, the first being the universality of Christianity. Jesus seemed to initially confine his message to Israel: "I was only sent to the lost sheep of Israel" (Matt 15:24), and he added an identical message to his disciples (Matt 10:6). It was only after the Resurrection that the particular changed to the universal: "go and make disciples of all nations" (Matt 28:19; see also Mark 16:15). Secondly, Mackintosh refers to the universal purpose of Christ's death, and especially the many hints in the fourth gospel such as: "so that the world may believe that you have sent me" (John 17:21).

Finally, Mackintosh turns to universal salvation with the supportive passages that include: "And I, when I am lifted up from this earth, will draw all people to myself (John 12:32), and "God . . . may have mercy on them all" (Rom 11:32). Millard Erickson[22] segmented the concept even further, subsuming conversion, atonement, opportunity, explicit opportunity, reconciliation, pardon,

---

20. Geivett, "Misgivings" and "Openness," 26–37.
21. Mackintosh, "Universalism," 783–86.
22. Erickson, "The Extent of Atonement," 825–41.

and restoration under the universalism umbrella. In essence, Erickson is stating that the opportunity to repent, and salvation, extends to everyone either during this life or after death; ultimately all will be saved.

The notion that the path to salvation can continue after death was also discussed by Richard Bauckham[23] with regard to *apokatastasis* (vide supra). Whereas torment for the wicked may last aeons, it will not be endless and the soul remains free to repent: God is wholly good and wants to bring all back to himself. This sentiment is echoed by Robertson McQuilkin[24] who, drawing on 2 Tim 3:15–17: "The Holy Scriptures, which are able to make you wise for salvation", noted that God revealed himself in the Bible for the purpose of human salvation. However, knowing that being saved is the free gift through faith, is not an excuse for inactivity or moral failure.[25]

What can we conclude from these various views on our freedom to take moral decisions, and whether or not these will comply with biblical edicts? We are probably on weak ground if we claim support for a conclusion that whatever we do will still result in God's approval; statements such as that referring to those who did not supply food for the hungry: "they will go away to eternal punishment, but the righteous shall have eternal life" (Matt 25:46) appear to leave no doubt that those who do wrong will be condemned. In contrast, those passages that do suggest that all shall be saved require a more liberal interpretation, and a belief in an omnipotent God whose love ensures that none will refuse to repent in the end.[26] This sentiment is echoed by others, including Harold Lindsell[27] who opines that to limit salvation to those who have heard the Gospel is unacceptable, Pinnock (in Geivett, 1998)[28] who queried whether God would cast into hell the majority who,

23. Bauckham, "Universalism," 47–54.

24. McQuilkin, *Understanding and Applying the Bible*.

25. Butler," Salvation," 550–51.

26. Bauckham, "Universalism," 47–54.

27. Lindsell, "Universalism today," 209–17.

28. Geivett, Geivett, "Misgivings" and "Openness," 26–37.

through no fault of their own, have not had the opportunity to become Christians, and Richard Mayhue[29] who said that eternal torment is cruel and incompatible with God's love and mercy.

Thus we have the view that we shall have to pay a heavy price for making the wrong moral decisions, as held by a number of scholars including Mayhue,[30] who suggested that what the Bible says about eternal punishment is correct, and Erickson[31] who concluded that God will reluctantly let the wicked perish. However, the words of Robert Mackintosh[32] penned many years earlier seem to be a more fitting conclusion. He wrote: "I could leave no child of mine to endless misery. Can God do that? We can only raise the question, our maker must answer it."

29. Mayhue, "Hell: Never, Forever," 129–45.
30. Ibid.
31. Erickson, "The extent of atonement," 825–41.
32. Mackintosh, "Universalism," 783–86.

CHAPTER 8

TAKING CHRISTIAN DECISIONS

THE DISCUSSION IN THE previous two chapters on the freedom to take our own decisions, and whether or not salvation is universal regardless of our actions on this earth, did not provide specific guidance for Christians when faced with moral issues such as suicide and euthanasia. Nor did it provide very much in the way of comfort for those who despair when life's burden becomes intolerable. Whilst the present chapter will attempt to be more helpful in this regard, it will not be prescriptive, and it will still require the reader to form his or her own opinion on the freedom that Christians have to take ethical decisions.

The Ten Commandments, including "Thou shalt not kill" (Ex 20:13, King James' Version, perhaps rendered more appropriately "You shall not murder", NIV), are not "laws" carrying prescribed punishments but are decrees, which refer to behavior that God wishes us to follow. Mosaic Law does not prohibit killing in war or self-defense, and the Old Testament cites at least ten transgressions, other than murder, which were punishable by death.[1] To give just two examples: "If a man commits adultery with another man's wife . . . both . . . are to be put to death" (Lev 10:10); and "Anyone who curses their father or mother is to be put to death" (Ex 21:17). Such examples of capital punishment were clearly regarded as not being murder, but as complying with God's word.

---

1. Holmes, *Ethics: Approaching moral decisions*

Thus, unlike the decrees, many of the Laws of Moses such as the two just mentioned, and with others listed in the book of Deuteronomy, do include sanctions. For example the penalty for a man falsely accusing his new wife of not being a virgin is a fine of one hundred shekels, whilst the punishment for the woman, if no proof can be found of her virginity, is being stoned to death (Deut 22: 19–21). Of course, some of the Decalogue items, including murder and stealing, have been universally absorbed into state laws, but others such as not coveting what your neighbor has remain just edicts. Likewise the Beatitudes listed by Jesus in his Sermon on the Mount are examples of virtuous behavior that pleases God, for example being merciful, and pure in heart (Matt 5:7–8; some paralleled in Luke 16:17–49 "Sermon on the Plain")[2].

Whilst the Decalogue probably remains the most widely quoted Old Testament guide to moral behavior, additional points of reference to ethics appear in the book of Proverbs and those of the prophets.[3] Scattered over several chapters of the book of Deuteronomy are the 613 laws of Moses, which seem to have been expanded from the original Ten Commandments to cover a great number of very specific situations. The Israelites were on their way to the Promised Land, discipline needed to be maintained, and their faith must not weaken despite the hardships.[4] Thus, Christopher Wright[5] concludes that Old Testament ethics evolved within a specific and context-bound situation, but Hock[6] mentions that, whether they were a pronouncement of law in a story, proverb or precept, they were principles cradled within God's redemptive plan.

The on-going relevance of the commandments is emphasized by the fact that all of them are referred to in total, or by strong implication, in more than one book of the New Testament. To cite just the example of murder, Matthew 5:21 quotes Jesus as saying

2. Ibid.
3. Ibid.
4. Hock, "Theology and Ethics," 33–48.
5. Wright, "Ethical Authority of the Old Testament," 101–20.
6. Hock, "Theology and Ethics," 38.

that "anyone who murders will be subject to judgment", and he confirms this commandment, along with others, again later (19:18). The same list is paralleled in Mark 10:19 and Luke 18:20. Paul reiterates this and other commandments in his letter to the Romans 13:9, adding significantly that all the prohibitions can be summarized by the command to love one's neighbor as oneself.

The New Testament contains a range of pronouncements on moral behavior, in addition to those that reflect the Decalogue. Evan Hock[7] states that, in general terms, ethics must be witness to God's will, as is indicated by several texts including John 14:21 "Whoever has my commands and keeps them is the one who loves me", and Luke 11:28 "Blessed rather are those who hear the word of God and obey it." Relevant passages are also found in Matthew 5:16 "let your light shine before others, that they may see your good deeds and glorify your Father in heaven", and 7:21 "Not everyone will enter the kingdom of heaven, but only the one who does the will of my father who is in heaven."

Whilst it is appropriate that our behavior should indeed reflect God's will, in the current issue of assisted dying it would be useful to know just what God's will is on this. If we are unsure, we are not alone, for Hock reminds us that the writer of Hebrews admonishes his audience by stating: "you need someone to teach you the elementary truths of God's word all over again" (5:12). However, the statement by Jesus when he was asked which the most important commandment was is unambiguous, with the exhortation to love the Lord and love our neighbor. Jesus emphasized the importance by adding that all the law and the prophets hang on these two (Matt, 22:37–40).

The Sermon on the Mount embraces commandments three, six and seven (you shall not misuse the Lord's name; shall not murder; shall not commit adultery). It also includes what has become known as the "golden rule": "so in everything, do to others what you would have them do to you, for this sums up the Law and the prophets." (Matt 7:12, paralleled in Luke 6: 31). Whilst this seems

7. Ibid., 33–48.

a useful and universal principle, Millard Erickson[8] comments that it was not addressed to the entire world, but only to Jesus' disciples. He adds that it can become "a powerful obstacle in the way of moral advance", because you might have some vices such as substance abuse or alcoholism, and be glad when somebody offers you your favorite (harmful) substance. It would be clearly wrong if you were to encourage another to be a drug addict by offering that person the same material. Only by considering the doctrine behind the rule does it become a guide for virtuous behavior.

Thus the "golden rule" example highlights the misunderstanding that can result from taking a text out of context in order to try and support a particular standpoint. The situation today is very different from what it was at the time of writing. We are separated from biblical times by cultural distance, geographical distance, and language distance, as well as being influenced by our own pre-understandings.[9] Using the Laws of Moses as contained in Exodus and Deuteronomy as examples, David Payne[10] explains that the words recorded were not intended to be timeless truths, but to address specific situations. God gave the guidance and direction necessary at the particular time. Payne adds that, as times change the guidance needs to be reconsidered to apply to the new circumstances—the Bible is not a fixed code of unchangeable laws.

8. Erickson, *Christian Theology*, 111.

9. Kline et al., *Introduction to Biblical Interpretation*, 14–15; 115.

10. Payne, *Deuteronomy*.

CHAPTER 9

OLD TESTAMANT REFERENCES TO ASSISTED DYING

A TRAWL THROUGH THE Old Testament canon yields few narratives that specifically concern suicide or euthanasia, and those that are reported are described without any comment on the moral rightness or wrongness of the incidents. There are, however, a number of texts that may provide advice, help and ethical guidance when a premature ending of life is being contemplated due to situations that have become difficult to endure. In the interests of completeness, all available references will be mentioned in either this chapter or the next, so that the reader can draw inspiration from where he or she finds it, although later chapters will revisit some of these examples in more detail. The citations are presented in the order that they chronologically appear in the Bible (or the first mention if paralleled elsewhere).

Twenty-one passages relating to assisted dying or despair have been identified in the Old Testament, with the prohibition on murder (Ex 20:13) having already been mentioned several times. The second reference is in Numbers 11:15, when Moses is troubled by the burden of leadership of the Israelites, including that he cannot fulfill the people's demand for food. He says to God "If this is how you are going to treat me, please go ahead and kill me right now". God does not kill Moses but shares some of the leadership burden with others, and provides quail for the people to eat. Later, Moses had stern words with the Israelites, as stated in Deuteronomy chapter 30, saying that he is giving them a choice between life and prosperity on the one hand, and death and destruction on the other (v. 15), depending on whether they obey God's commands or turn away from him. Moses urges the people to choose life so that they and their children may live (v. 19).

A clear case of euthanasia is reported in Judges 9:53–54 where Abimelek who, with his invading forces, was responsible for many deaths. He was about to set fire to a tower in Thebez that contained people who were hiding there, but a woman dropped a millstone on his head and cracked his skull. Abimelek called his amour-bearer and asked him to finish him off with his sword, so nobody could say that a woman had killed him. The servant ran him through, and Abimelek died. Verse fifty-four states that God had thus repaid Abimelek's wickedness. Later in Judges there is an example of suicide that should strictly speaking be regarded self-sacrifice.

Chapter 16:28–30 report the death of Samson in the temple. This hero, who had battled the Philistines, had been captured and blinded by them, and was tied to the two central pillars of the temple. Samson prayed to the Lord asking for strength, and then said: "Let me die with the Philistines." He then pushed down the two central pillars of the temple containing Philistines, thereby destroying the building and the Philistines, but also ending his own life.

The death of Saul has some parallels to that of Abimelek (vide supra). Saul, who had been seriously wounded by the Philistines, asked his amour-bearer to kill him by running him through with his sword and thus deny the heathen enemy the pleasure of doing so. When the servant declined, Saul fell on his own sword and died; the amour-bearer then followed suit, resulting in a double suicide (1 Sam 31:4–5). Interestingly, the story continues in 2 Samuel but with a different ending. This time the man previously described as the amour-bearer, but now as an Amalekite, does not join Saul in suicide but goes to David and tells him how he had complied with the wounded Saul's wishes and dispatched him.

Despite what might be seen as an act of compassion, David has the Amalekite killed (1: 15). Thus it is not clear whether the example of Saul should be regarded as suicide or active euthanasia. Because of the two differing reports, we can not be sure of the true facts, but it remains a possibility that the Amalekite did not kill Saul out of compassion, or perhaps did not even have a hand in this deed; when reporting the events to David, he may have anticipated that he might receive some praise and reward.

The Second Book of Samuel also relates an elaborate story of a plot to capture King David by Absalom, who was a son of David but had rebelled against him. Ahithophel, who was a one-time counselor to David but had also now turned against him, advised Absalom to raise an army and pursue the King. However, Hushai, who was a friend of David, gave different advice to Absalom; this was followed and it allowed David to escape. Chapter 17, verse twenty-three reads: "When Ahithophel saw that his advice had not been followed . . . he put his house in order and hanged himself."

The next example, in 1 Kings chapter 19, does not describe an actual death but a death wish. Elijah had challenged 450 prophets of Baal to prove that their god could create a fire and burn up a sacrifice. The prophets failed in this task, but Elijah succeeded by praying to the God of Israel. Following this test, Elijah killed all the Baal prophets. Elijah was reported to Jezebel, and he ran away to the wilderness, feeling threatened. Verse four states: "he . . . prayed that he might die. 'I have had enough, Lord,' he said. 'Take my life; I am no better than my ancestors.'" His plea was not complied with, and he continued with further adventures.

Another person (assuming he was a person, and that the story was not symbolic of the exiled Jews per se) who wished he were dead was Job, normally an upright man of God before he was tested by Satan, and everything started going wrong. Job laments his situation and says "Oh, that I might have my request . . . that God would be willing to crush me, to let loose his hand and cut off my life!" (Job 6:8–9). He repeats this sentiment in the next chapter with: "I will speak out in the anguish of my spirit", adding "I prefer strangling and death, rather than this body of mine, I despise my life; I would not live for ever." (7:15–16). Once again his request was not honored, and Job later made his peace with the Lord.

Seven references to despair and potential end of life situations occur in the book of Psalms, although they are not specifically linked to suicide or euthanasia. The Psalms were probably written over quite a long period of time, including the Israeli monarchic era during that nation's rise to power, which dates from around 1,000 to 745 BC. Some Psalms are ascribed to named individuals, for example David, and different categories can be distinguished such as the greatness of God, laments, thanksgiving, and the king. Psalms were no doubt intended to be sung, as musical directions are sometimes included, and there may have been different purposes for different Psalms, for example prayer, praise, or teaching[1]. Jesus and the disciples were known to sing: "When they had sung a hymn, they went out to the Mount of Olives" (Matt 26:30/ Mark 14:26).

In the following summary, the commentary by J. A. Motyer[2] will be drawn on for background details where applicable. The first example is from Psalm 13, which is ascribed to David, and concerns a plea to God that he has not been forgotten during his time of trial with his foes. Verse three reads "Give light to my eyes, or I will sleep in death." Psalm 34, also ascribed to David, concerns his captivity and subsequent escape with the Lord's help. David rejoices that God protects, and states: "The righteous person may have many troubles, but the Lord delivers him from them all; he protects all his bones, not one of them will be broken." (vv. 19–20). Psalm 90 is described as a prayer of Moses, who laments that life comes to an end because we are sinful beings. He states in verse ten: "Our days may come to seventy years, or eighty, if our strength endures; yet the best of them are but trouble and sorrow, for they quickly pass and we fly away."

The fourth example concerns Psalm 118, which Motyer lists as being one of 'The Egyptian Hallel: A cantata of salvation' (Psalms 113–118), those that formed part of the Passover celebration. He states that Jesus and his disciples would have sung these at the Last Supper (see Matt 26:30, vide supra). Verse seventeen

1. Motyer, "The Psalms," 485–583.
2. Ibid.

states: "I will not die but live, and will proclaim what the Lord has done." Motyer interprets this as meaning that death will not have the last word. The notion that God will protect during difficult and dangerous times continues in Psalm 138, another example of one ascribed to David. Verse seven reads: "Though I walk in the midst of trouble, you preserve my life."

Psalm 139, also of David, acknowledges God's complete knowledge of him: "if I settle on the far side of the sea, even there your hand will guide me, your right hand will hold me fast." (vv. 9–10). In verse thirteen David says: "For you created my inmost being; you knit me together in my mother's womb". Whilst these passages suggest that David will be protected from danger, they also suggest determinism as opposed to freedom, including the time and nature of David's death. Finally, Psalm 147:3 reads: "He heals the broken and binds up their wounds" and, in verse six, "The Lord sustains the humble but casts the wicked to the ground." This hymn of praise emphasizes God's concern with the physical and spiritual needs of individuals.

Continuing now with references in Old Testament books that chronologically follow Psalms, Ecclesiastes commences with a statement that the words are from a teacher, son of David (v. 1). Chapter 7:16–17 states: "Do not be over-righteous, neither be otherwise—why destroy yourself? Do not be overwicked, and do not be a fool—why die before your time?" However, this may not necessarily mean actually taking one's life. The book of Jeremiah describes how the prophet had been beaten and put in the stocks for prophesizing God's pending destruction of Israel, and he laments about his mistreatment. He cursed the day he was born (20:14), and regrets that God did not kill him in his mother's womb (v.17), and questions why he ever came out of the womb only to see trouble and sorrow (v. 18). Later in his book, after Israel had been invaded and the people exiled, believing that they would become extinct, Jeremiah writes to them and recounts what God had said to him, namely: "For I know the plans I have for you . . . plans to prosper you and not harm you" (29:11).

The final Old Testament reference to be cited here is from Jonah 4:3, and is a more obvious death wish. He says: "Now, Lord, take away my life, for it is better for me to die than to live." In verse eight he repeats that "it would be better for me to die than to live." Jonah said this because he expected God to destroy Nineveh, the enemy of Israel, and he had reluctantly visited that city at God's request to preach against them. However, the king of Nineveh heeded the warning and instructed the nation to give up their evil ways. God then relented and did not destroy them. Jonah sulked because the destruction about which he warned did not materialize, and he then lost his purpose for living. God did not let him die, but instead tried to reason with him.

A summary of the categories of Old Testament references to end of life issues is shown in Table 1. It will be seen that one is a command not to kill, four relate to euthanasia or suicide (one being a double suicide), five concern death wishes or a wish that one had never been born, one is an offer of a choice between life and death, one is a person being killed, one is a lament that life comes to an end, one is a warning not to destroy the self with bad behavior, and the remaining seven concern God's protection of the faithful from danger.

Table 1: Summary of Old Testament references to end of life

Category	Bible references
Commandment	Ex 20:13
Actual suicide	Judg 16:19–30; 1 Sam 31:4–5; 2 Sam 17:23
Euthanasia request/ death wish	Num 11:10–15; Judg 9:53–4; 1 Kgs 19:4; Job 6:8–9; 7:15–16; Jer 20:14–18;
Amalekite killed	Jon 4:3–8
Lament about end of life	2 Sam 1:9–10
Choice between life and death	Ps 90:10
Warning not to destroy self	Deut 30:15–19
God protects the faithful	Ecc 7:16–17; Jer 29:11; Ps 13:3; Ps 34:19–20; Ps 118:17; Ps 138:7; Ps 139:9–13; Ps 147:3; 6

CHAPTER 10

NEW TESTAMENT REFERENCES
TO ASSISTED DYING

A TOTAL OF THIRTY references in the New Testament to end of life matters or despairing situations have been cited by various commentators, and again all will be mentioned without too much concern for the level of helpfulness at this stage, so that the reader can draw his of her own inferences. As previously, they will be presented in the order in which they appear in the New Testament.

The first three references are taken from Matthew, commencing with 6:34 that is part of the passage on Jesus' Sermon on the Mount: "do not worry about tomorrow, for tomorrow will worry about itself". A little later, Jesus says to his disciples as he sends them out: "Whoever finds their life will lose it, and whoever loses their life for my sake will find it." (Matt 10:39). Richard France[1] considers this to be the language of martyrdom. Next is a specific reference to an act of suicide. Judas had betrayed Jesus and received thirty pieces of silver for doing this. However, when he saw that Jesus had been condemned to death he was filled with remorse. Matthew 27:5 states: "So Judas threw the money into the temple and left. Then he went away and hanged himself." (27:5). However, this is reported differently in Acts 1:18: "With the payment he received for his wickedness, Judas bought a field; there he fell headlong, his body burst open and all his intestines spilled out."

1. France, "Matthew," 904–45.

Mark 5:1–10 reports an example of self-harm, with the story of the demon- possessed man named Legion, who cried out and cut himself with stones. Jesus exorcised the demons. The same book in a supplementary section not included in all manuscripts, quotes Jesus' words to the disciples when he appeared to them after his resurrection: "Whoever believes and is baptized will be saved, but whoever does not believe will be condemned" (16:16). The nature of the "condemnation" is not made explicit. The literal Greek translation of *katakrinō* is "to condemn or pass judgement",[2] but some translations prefer alternatives such as: "shall be damned" (21st Century King James' version), and "shall be judged and punished" (Worldwide English version).

Scholars have nominated only one reference from Luke's gospel that provides guidance on coping with life's difficulties. Jesus tells his disciples the story of the persistent widow who persevered in her mission to seek justice, despite many refusals, and was eventually rewarded. Luke 18:1 reports Jesus as saying: "they should always pray and never give up."

John's gospel contains five references to coping with adversity. In 10:10 Jesus says in his story of the good shepherd: "The thief comes lonely to steal and kill and destroy; I have come that they may have life." Continuing with the simile of the sheep, he reiterates this again in 10:28: "I give them eternal life, and they shall never perish; no one will snatch them out of my hand." In John 12:25 Jesus says: "Anyone who loves their life will lose it, while anyone who hates their life in this world will keep it for eternal life" and, in 14:1, there are the following words of comfort: "Do not let your hearts be troubled." Equally comforting for the despairing is "Anyone who loves me will obey my teaching. My Father will love them, and we will come to them and make our home with them." (14:23). Some regard Jesus' death on the cross as being an act of suicide, or perhaps martyrdom. John's gospel 10:18 reports: "No one takes [my life] from me, but I lay it down of my own accord." However, this example will not be pursued further in the present book.

2. Friberg et al., *Analytical Lexicon of the Greek New Testament*, 218.

The book of Acts 16:27 contains a case of an intended suicide. Paul, Silas and others were in prison when an earthquake released the prisoners' chains. On seeing this, the jailor drew his sword and was about to kill himself, but Paul talked him out of it. Four quotations appear in Romans, the first being in Chapter 6 where Paul is saying that believers have been joined with Christ, including his death: "For we know that our old self was crucified with him so that the body ruled by sin might be done away with . . . because anyone who has died has been set free from sin." (6:6–7). Paul continues in similar vein in 8:38–39: "For I am convinced that neither death nor life . . . will be able to separate us from the love of God that is in Christ Jesus our Lord."

Discouragement from the need to contemplate suicide but to trust in God emerges in several references, not the least in statements by Paul. In Romans 10:13 he says: "For everyone who calls on the name of the Lord will be saved." Likewise, in 12:2: "Do not conform to the pattern of this world . . . then you will be able to test and approve what God's will is." Paul continues with the notion of God's protection in 1 Corinthians 3:16–17: "Don't you know that you yourselves are God's temple and that God's spirit lives among you? If anyone destroys God's temple, God will destroy that person." He repeats the metaphor in 6:19: "Do you not know that your bodies are temples of the Holy Spirit?"

In his second letter to the Corinthians, Paul again reminds his readers of God's presence during time of trial: "We are hard pressed on every side, but not crushed . . . struck down but not destroyed. We always carry around in our body the death of Jesus, so that the life of Jesus may also be revealed in our body."(4:8–9). Also in the second letter, Paul talks about a "thorn in his flesh" (a messenger from Satan) that he pleaded with God to remove. God replied "My grace is sufficient for you, for my power is made perfect in weakness." (12:9).

In his letter to the Ephesians, Paul also raised the topic with his reference to predestination: "For he chose us . . . he predestined us for adoption to sonship through Jesus Christ, in accordance with his pleasure and will." (1:4–5). As discussed in Chapter 6 of the present book, the implication is that if all is pre-ordained, we do not need to agonize over any decision regarding the premature ending of our own life or the life of others. This is hinted again by Paul in his letter to the Philippians 1:6: "being confident of this, that he who began a good work in you will carry it on to completion until the day of Christ Jesus." Later in the chapter Paul becomes rather more specific, and he muses on whether or not it is worth him continuing to live: "If I am to go on living in the body, this will mean fruitful labor for me. Yet what shall I choose? I do not know! . . . I desire to depart and be with Christ . . . but it is more necessary for you that I remain in the body." (1:22–24). However, he does ultimately decide to remain "in the body" (v. 25).[3]

The writer of Hebrews provides three possible references. He or she appears to be addressing a Christian group who were experiencing challenges to their faith, and is encouraging them not to capitulate. The first reference 10:32–36 states: "you endured in a great conflict and suffering . . . you suffered along with those in prison . . . you need to persevere so that when you have done the will of God, you will receive what he has promised you." The writer continues by reviewing the many who had lived by their faith despite being persecuted, and states: "These were all commended for their faith . . . since God had planned something better for us so that only together with us would they be made perfect." (11:39–40). Finally, the writer quotes Psalm 118, saying: "The Lord is my helper; I will not be afraid. What can mere mortals do to me?" (13:6).

The first letter from Peter also urges people to be strong in the face of adversity, as well as not claiming to be superior: "Humble yourselves, therefore, under God's mighty hand, that he may lift you up in due time. Cast all your anxiety on him because he cares for you." (1 Pet 5:6–7). In the first letter of John, lack of love is likened to death: "We know that we have passed from death to life, because we love each other. Anyone who does not love remains in death." (3:14–15).

3. Essex, "Euthanasia," 192–215.

A more specific reference to death occurs in Revelation, but it is a case of death being denied. For those who were tortured because they did not have the sign of God on their foreheads, the writer states: "During these days people will seek death but will not find it; they will long to die, but death will elude them." (9:6). The final New Testament reference also comes from Revelation, and is much concerned with the judgment of the dead but in the pictorial and symbolic language typical of this book. Chapter 20, verse twelve states: "And I saw the dead, great and small, standing before the throne, and the books were opened . . . The dead were judged according to what they had done as recorded in the books."

A summary of these thirty New Testament references to end of life issues is shown in Table 2. Whilst the categories are not always specific, they have been divided into three actual or potential suicides or self-harm, three condemnations of inappropriate conduct, three exhortations not to give in, four suggestions that our actions are predestined, two that death will be denied, and one that lack of love is equivalent to death. The remaining fourteen all reflect the notion that believers need not worry because they will be protected; they should remain strong, trust God, and pray in times of trial.

Table 2: Summary of New Testament references to end of life

Category	Bible references
Actual or potential suicide; self-harm	Matt 27:5; Mark 5:1–10; Acts:16:27
Unbelieving and selfish behavior condemned	Matt 10:39; Mark 16:16; Jn 12:25
Be strong, avoid capitulation	Luk 18:1; Heb 10:32–36; 1Pet 5:6–7
Life is predestined	Eph 1:4–5; Phil 1:6; Phil 1:22–24;
Death denied/the dead will be judged	Heb 11:39; Rev 9:6; Rev 20:12
Lack of love is like death	1 Jn 3:14–15
Don't worry, believers will not perish but will be protected	Mat 6:34; Jn 10:10; Jn 10:28, Jn 14:1; Jn 14:23; Rom 6:6–7; Rom 8:38–39; Rom 10:13; Rom 12:2; 1 Cor 3:16–17; 1 Cor 6:19; 2 Cor 4:8–9; 2 Cor 12:9; Heb 13:6

CHAPTER 11

ARGUMENTS FOR AND AGAINST
SUICIDE AND EUTHANASIA

TURNING NOW TO THE extreme situation where death is contemplated, are there any ethical principles in the Bible that can inform on the freedom to decide when to die, and passages that suggest what God wishes in these cases? As discussed in chapters 9 and 10, there are only a few examples in the Bible that refer directly to suicide or euthanasia. The Old Testament citations comprised the wounded Abimelek who had his servant finish him off (Judges 9:53–54), and Samson who brought down the temple, thus killing the Philistine enemies as well as himself (Judges 16:30), although this should probably be regarded as an instance self-sacrifice or martyrdom.

Then there is Saul who asked his amour-bearer to kill him but, when the servant would not do so, he took his own life (1 Sam 31:5). This appears to be a clear case of suicide, but it is less certain whether or not the amour-bearer also took his own life in view of the version in 2 Samuel (1:15–16). Here he is referred to as an Amalekite who reported to King David that he had dispatched Saul at the latter's request (which would be an act of euthanasia), only to have him, the Amalekite, put to death on David's command for killing the "Lord's anointed." Finally, there is Ahithophel who hanged himself when his advice to capture David was not followed (2 Sam 17:23).

In the New Testament, chapter 10 only cited one confirmed suicide, that of Judas who is reported to have hanged himself (Matt

27:5), although in Acts 1:18 it is stated that he fell and his body burst open. Some regard Jesus' death on the cross as being an example of suicide, although more correctly martyrdom as he said that he gives up his life of his own free will (John 10:18). Finally, Paul seemed to have been contemplating suicide so that he can meet his savior, when he wrote: " . . . I desire to depart and be with Christ . . . but it is more necessary for you that I remain in the body . . . " (Phil 1:23–24), but he decides to remain alive (v. 25).[1]

In each of the five examples, the scriptures appear to remain morally neutral, although the death of Abimelek is regarded as a just reward for his evil ways. There is also a rather cryptic hint in Romans 5:7 when Paul writes "Very rarely will anyone die for a righteous person, although for a good person someone might possibly dare to die."[2] The precise meaning of this verse is disputed, but one possibility is that it refers to dying for a good cause rather than a good person.[3] If this is the case, it might suggest that there are some cases where a form of self-sacrifice is justified or acceptable.

Although it would be helpful to try and debate this issue neatly in terms of clear-cut arguments, in practice there are many gray areas mostly based on just which category of assisted dying one is considering, such as active, passive, voluntary and involuntary. Obviously an involuntary/active ending of a life would be far more ethically problematic than would a voluntary/passive one but, as noted more recently by Thomas Schreiner,[4] "the culture of death that promotes euthanasia under the guise of compassion and personal right, may confuse some in the church."

Commencing with some arguments put forward that oppose assisted dying, it is clear that the attitude to suicide has varied over the years, but one early opponent was Saint Augustine (354–430). Robin Gill[5] explains that Augustine regarded it as an

1. Essex, "Euthanasia," 192–215.
2. Bruinsma, *Matters of Life and Death.*
3. Schreiner, *Romans.*
4. Schreiner, "Importance of Ethics," 2.
5. Gill, *Textbook of Christian Ethics.*

act of murder, and that nobody has a private right to kill anybody, including the self. He did not regard suicide as showing a great spirit, but as a weakness in the face of oppression, and he ridiculed it as a means to avoid evil. The commandment not to kill does not allow for any exception, unless permitted by the law of God. This view was obviously taken seriously in Britain in the Middle Ages, when it was forbidden to give a Christian burial to suicide victims. As mentioned in chapter 1, Britain only decriminalized suicide in the year 1961.

A conservative view of suicide is described by J. P. Moreland[6] as a violation of one's sanctity-of-life duty to respect oneself as an end and not a means. One's duty is to God, the giver of life, who gives purpose to life in the midst of hardships. Michael Mckenzie[7] points out that those who hold the strongest views against suicide, or any other premature ending of a life, are the Scriptural Ethicists. They regard such acts as breaking the sixth Commandment and taking upon themselves the prerogative that belongs only to God (see also Cook, 1992).[8] This applies equally to anyone, including medical staff, who may assist a person who wishes to end his or her life. To do otherwise would violate God's standards. But what if the person is an atheist? Mckenzie states that the Scriptural Ethicists maintain that every effort should be made to evangelize that individual in order to avoid their eternal suffering in the afterlife.

Garry Stewart[9] also propounds a hard-line view, lamenting that contemporary society is drifting away from truth and the God of the Bible, replacing it with relativism, self-indulgence and the "right to die" philosophy. The fact that we are created in God's image (Gen 1 26–28) means that we must therefore represent him in this world. We can never know what his purpose is for each of us, and any thoughts that we would be better off without the Lord are erroneous. Stewart cites Viktor Frankl who, though imprisoned in the notorious Auschwitz death camp, never ceased to maintain

6. Moreland, "Morality of Suicide," 221.

7. Mckenzie, "Christian Norms in the Ethical Square," 413–28.

8. Cook, *The Moral Maze*.

9. Stewart, "Suicide and the Christian Worldview," 203–19.

that life continues to have meaning even in the most extreme suffering (this was also confirmed by Frankl at a lecture in 1985, attended by the present writer).

It might be expected that the Roman Catholic Church would hold conservative views on this topic, relying as it does on Papal decrees for guidance. Whilst reiterating the official policy and professing that life is a gift from God and must be endured to the end, Hans Küng,[10] who is himself a Roman Catholic priest, is also prepared to consider that our theological task should be to remove suffering as far as possible. He concludes that the all-merciful God has left dying people the responsibility for decisions about their own death, and Küng has the courage to state that the encyclical that opposes this is cold and pitiless. Thus, under appropriate circumstances, he would regard certain forms of passive euthanasia as surrendering one's life back to God.

Whilst Küng might be less rigid, a more orthodox Roman Catholic stand is made by Kathryn Holewa.[11] She tries to remain faithful to the second Vatican Council's condemnation of euthanasia, but her selectivity of supporting evidence and sometimes contradictory statements are suggestive of an inward struggle with this issue. Whilst condemning euthanasia as a means to avoid suffering, she is quite happy to advocate palliative care to the dying for this very same purpose, and she respects the patient's self-determination of the level of care administered to them. She also states that life should not be extended by disproportionate means.

Turning now to arguments that support a more liberal approach to this dilemma, whilst Millard Erickson[12] is not primarily a supporter of assisted dying, he does include some instances that would not result in condemnation. For example, he states that many Christians would have no ethical objections to passive euthanasia such as withholding treatment, or even "fully utilizing" pain killers with the knowledge that this may hasten death. Love and compassion should permit a person of sound mind to seek

10. Küng, "A Dignified Dying?" 381–87.

11. Holewa, "Palliative Care," 208–21.

12. Erickson, "Euthanasia and Christian Ethics," 15–24.

medical help to facilitate an easy death, in the spirit of "Blessed are the merciful, for they will be shown mercy" (Matt 5:7). A similar tolerant view is voiced by J. P. Moreland, [13] based on a person's right to autonomy and quality of life considerations, especially if it relates to passive euthanasia.

A key consideration is to balance the downside of helping someone to die, with that of permitting more suffering.[14] Life is not just a matter of "quantity" (that is, longevity) but also "quality". If a person feels he or she no longer has any self-worth or contribution to make, and is fully dependent on others, then Cook asks if compassion should include permanently relieving the pain and agony of that individual? If the person wants to take his or her own life in an act of suicide, then beneficence should be relegated to the relatively minor role of attempting to dissuade that person; if this fails, then it would be right for outside parties to step aside.[15] Mckenzie cautions that if Scriptural Ethicists continue to be reluctant to rely on anything but scripture to support their opposition to any form of assisted dying, then it would not be surprising if medical technology continues to have little patience with them.

Passive euthanasia includes the withholding life-sustaining nutrients, for example in the case of a person who is in a persistent vegetative state (PVS). Gilbert Meilaender[16] on the one hand states that even if a person remains as such to the extent that he or she is comatose, we still have an obligation to continue feeding them. On the other hand, he concedes that such a person may be "trying to die", and that by continuing to feed them we are not allowing this to happen. Robert Rakestraw[17] takes this argument further when he queries the definition of "personhood". If this means that we are made in the image of God (Gen 1:26) and that we are his representatives on earth, then an individual who is in a PVS can

13. Moreland, "Morality of Suicide," 214–31.

14. Cook, *The Moral Maze*.

15. Mckenzie, "Christian Norms and the Ethical Square," 413–28.

16. Meilaender, "On Removing Food and Water," 109–116.

17. Rakestraw, "Persistent Vegetative State," 116–131.

no longer fulfill this role. Thus the withholding of nutrient would be justified.

An Adventist view put forward by Reinder Bruinsma[18] includes the notion that, whilst love usually means that we defend life, it may not exclude the ending of a life under certain circumstances. He notes that we are promised eternal life in the next world, so Christians do not need to cling to the last vestiges of life in this one. Thus, life-extending medical treatments may be stopped if they needlessly prolong the process of dying. Finally, Norman Geisler[19] states that the arguments in favor of permitting active euthanasia include the moral right to die with dignity, that it is an act of mercy and compassion to the sufferer, and that it is the humane thing to do. Whilst he does not necessarily personally agree with this, Geisler concurs with Bruinsma that prolonging death through life-support can be seen as resisting the hand of God.

18. Bruinsma, *Matters of Life and Death*.
19. Geisler, *Christian Ethics*.

CHAPTER 12

THE OLD TESTAMENT'S ATTITUDE TOWARD LIFE AND DEATH

THE PREVIOUS CHAPTER DEALT with the more obvious biblical references to suicide and euthanasia, few though they are, and the opinions of commentators who either support or oppose any intervention that hastens the natural end of life. However, chapters 9 and 10 listed many more biblical references—fifty-one in total—that scholars have suggested provide advice or guidance on situations of despair, whether or not they include a desire to end it all. This chapter therefore puts aside the more specific "death" texts, and revisits the "secondary" ones to see if they can inform on how to combat a feeling of being unable to cope with life's adversities. We commence with those that appear in the Old Testament.

Four of the Old Testament citations reflect a death wish, but none were fulfilled by God, and a further two lament the writer's very existence. The first death wish concerns Moses' attempt to lead the Israelites on their journey, but the people were complaining again, this time because they only had manna to eat. They seemed to have forgotten that they were being delivered from Egypt, and disbelief was starting to spread. God became angry, and Moses lamented that his burden was heavy and that, if this was how God was going to treat him, he wished the Lord would kill him there and then (Num 11:10–15). The outcome was that Moses was not struck down, and that God provided quails and eggs to eat. Secondly, Elijah was in a state of despair, and feared for his life. He told God that he had had enough and wished to die (1 Kgs 19:4). As with Moses, his plea was again ignored, and instead God sent an angel to help Elijah on his way.

Job (assuming he was a real person, although the message would apply equally to the exiled Israelites as a whole) suffered a lot, and at first bore this calmly. As his distress continued he found it more difficult to tolerate it, and became angry with God for bringing this upon him. In 7:15–16 he despairs, saying that he would prefer to be strangled and die. He does not die, and he ultimately becomes reconciled with God again. Similarly, Jonah 4:3 pleads with God to end his life, and wishes he were dead (v. 9) because the Lord had changed his mind about destroying Nineveh. God questions Jonah's right to be angry, and explains why he had spared the city. Douglas Stuart[1] explains that this response is a message to all who would query the validity of God's decisions.

Whilst Jeremiah falls short of requesting death, because of the mistreatment he had received his faith is tested, and he curses the day he was born and that he was not killed in the womb (Jer 20:14; 17). Nevertheless, he continues with his mission to warn the people of Judah of the consequences of their apostasy, and he foretells the New Covenant. A similar lamentation is expressed by Moses (Psalm 90:10), in addition to the actual death wish mentioned in the Book of Numbers. He worked long and faithfully doing God's work, but complained that life is hard and comes to an end before we know it. Like Jeremiah, Moses still continued with his mission until his appointed time. In Psalm 13, David says he trusts God but still asks him for divine favor during his efforts to overcome his enemies or he will "sleep in death" (v. 3).

These references to a death wish, none of which were complied with, or pleas for God's help, suggest that no matter how bad our lives may be, asking God to end it is not the solution. None of those mentioned did actually attempt to commit suicide, despite the trials and tribulations they were experiencing. The message that emerges in each of these instances is to have faith, keep going, and ask for God's help.

1. Stuart, "Jonah," 814–21.

With the next batch of Old Testament references, of which all but one appear in the Book of Psalms, the theme is on how God protects the faithful. Thus, like those reviewed above, these passages should encourage those who despair to keep going rather than capitulate to thoughts of suicide. In Psalm 34 David says that being righteous does not mean that one is free from trouble but, if we pray for help, God will still protect and deliver us from adversity (verses 17–20). In the next example, the anonymous writer of Psalm 118 rejoices how God has protected him and helped him defeat his enemies. In verse seventeen, because of God's care he is able to say that he will not die but will live. Psalm 138:7 has David rejoicing that God has preserved his life during times of trouble and, in Psalm 139:7–12, he says that whatever he does and wherever he goes, the Lord guides and holds him fast.

This sentiment continues with Psalm 147:3;6 which, although anonymous, praises how God cares for both the spiritual (broken-hearted) and physical (binds their wounds) of the people, and sustains the humble (those of low status). The last example in this cluster is from Jeremiah 29:11, who writes to the Judeans exiled in Babylon who are obviously unhappy with their situation. He tells them that God has plans for them, plans that will prosper them and not harm them. Thus, this group of texts confirms the need to ask God's help and trust that he will guide and sustain, rather than give up.

The first of the two remaining Old Testament references is in Deuteronomy 30:15–17, and it quite simply preaches the message that one has a choice. Moses tells the assembled Israelites that they can either love and obey the Lord, and have life and prosperity, or turn away, be disobedient or worship other gods, and face death and destruction. There is no excuse; it is a straight choice. Finally, Ecclesiastes 7:16–17 reports someone quoting the words of a teacher. Michael Eaton[2] states that the message is addressed both to the pessimists and secularists of Israel, and to the faithful who do not take seriously the reality of life in this world. The passage exhorts the reader to not be over-righteous, and be neither foolish

2. Eaton, "Ecclesiastes," 609–18.

nor over-wicked; this just leads to destruction and death before the appointed time.

It thus appears that all the Old Testament references to life's difficulties that lead to despair and possible ending of life reflect a similar theme. This can be summarized as not giving up in times of difficulty, and having faith in God. The Lord does not respond to death wishes, but he protects the faithful and cares for the broken hearted. However, we have a choice: obey God and reap these benefits, or turn against him and face destruction.

CHAPTER 13

THE NEW TESTAMENT'S ATTITUDE TOWARD LIFE AND DEATH

THERE IS ONLY ONE report of an actual suicide in the New Testament among the thirty passages that have been suggested as relevant to despair and possible premature ending of a life, although Paul contemplates whether it would be better for him to die so that he could be with Christ (Phil 1:22–24). In Mark 5:1–10 there is the story of the demented man, Legion, who self-harmed and may have wished to end it all, but his demon was exorcised by Jesus. As with the Old Testament examples reviewed in the previous chapter, the remaining "secondary" references will now be examined to see what guidance they may offer to those who are finding it difficult to cope with their adversity. Where there are parallel versions in the Gospels, exegesis will concentrate on just the first citation that appears in the Bible.

Two references concern death wishes, the first being the story from Acts 16:25–27 where Paul and Silas were imprisoned. An earthquake caused the doors to fly open and the jailor thought the prisoners had escaped. He was about to kill himself but Paul stopped him and assured him that all were still there. John's vision in Revelation states that those people who were not servants of God would be tormented by stinging locusts for five months, to such an extent that they will seek death but will not find it; they will long to die but will instead live (9:4–6). In other words, they will have to suffer, but Craig Keener[1] suggests that the fact that a time limit is included may serve to allow for repentance. Thus, with these examples as with all the others, nobody actually dies. However, in Revelation 20:12, when people have already died, it is written that the dead were judged according to what they had done in life. The wicked would be thrown into the "lake of fire" (v.15).

The next three passages urge people to be strong and continue in the face of adversity. Luke 18:1 reports Jesus telling his disciples a parable illustrating that they should always pray and not give up. The parable concerns a widow who had to keep nagging a judge before he granted her justice (v. 5). Thus God will bring justice to his chosen ones but, like the widow, they may have to wait for it (v. 7). Does the reference to "chosen ones" imply that only the elect will be listened to? Leon Morris[2] debates this point and concludes that it may either mean that God is strengthening the elect, or that he is giving the wicked time to repent. In similar vein, the writer of Hebrews simply tells his readers, who presumably are facing opposition for their faith, that they should persevere so that, when they have done the will of God, they will receive what was promised (10:36). Likewise, Peter writes to the Christians who are scattered throughout Asia Minor, exhorting them to humble themselves and cast their anxiety on God, because he cares for them.

Three references refer to the condemnation of unbelieving behavior. Matthew 10:39 rather cryptically states that whoever finds their life will lose it, but whoever loses his life for Jesus' sake will find it. Craig Keener[3] explains that this passage means that we must love Jesus more than we do our own lives, even if this means being led away to execution. This is matched in John 12:24–25, with Jesus first saying that a seed must die—that is it ceases to be a seed—before it can grow and produce more seeds. This is then applied to people, in that anyone who loves their life will lose it but, if they hate their life in this world then they will keep it for eternity. Mark 16:16 quotes Jesus, after his resurrection, as saying

1. Keener, *Revelation,* 268–69.
2. Morris, *Luke.*
3. Keener, *Matthew,* 210.

that whoever believes and is baptized will be saved, but those who do not believe will be condemned. Baptism was to be a sign of commitment to Christ.[4]

In the first letter of John 3:14–15, the writer states that lack of love is like death, and that anyone who hates a brother or sister remains in death. The reference to death is an analogy for the state of an unbeliever, whereas life is what the believer gains.[5] The implication for those who consider ending it all because of their difficult situation is that love should guide the actions of both the person contemplating suicide, and the one who is asked to help them end their life.

Three references can be grouped under heading of predestination, which was discussed in chapter 7, and also hinted at earlier in the present chapter in Luke 18:1–7, with the story of the widow nagging for justice and Jesus' responding with a comment about "his chosen ones". In Ephesians 1:4–5 Paul writes that God chose us and predestined us for sonship in Christ—which can be interpreted as being our future full adoption as sons through Jesus Christ.[6] In his letter to the Philippians 1:6 Paul refers to God as being the one who began good work in them (as Christians), and will carry it forward to completion. The third reference is taken from the writer of Hebrews 11:39–40 who states that God had planned something better for the Old Testament faithful, but they had never received what was promised. However, we now have the experience of the coming of the Messiah, so that only together with him would they enjoy perfection.

The final fourteen of the New Testament citations, nearly half of the total, reflect the notion that the believer will not perish. Matthew has a whole sub-section of the Sermon on the Mount headed: "Do not worry" (6:25–34), which concerns assurances that God will provide for our essential needs. Jesus exhorts the people not to worry about tomorrow because tomorrow will take care of itself (v.

---

4. Cole, "Mark," 946–77.

5. Morris, "1 John," 1397–1409.

6. Turner, "Ephesians," 1222–44.

34). In commenting on this passage, Craig Keener[7] notes that the lesson we can learn is that anxiety will not add even a moment to one's life; in the fast-paced contemporary culture a troubled heart can actually shorten life. Two separate verses in John chapter 10 refer to the good shepherd and the sheep. Verse nine quotes Jesus as saying that he is the gate for the sheep, and whoever enters through him will be saved. Further on, in verse twenty-eight, he adds that he will give them (the sheep) eternal life and they will never perish. This is in contrast to the false shepherds who just bring death.

John has another two relevant verses in chapter 14. Verse one succinctly cites Jesus telling his disciples, who are worried about the consequences of his betrayal, that they should not let their hearts be troubled; he would return and bring them to him (v. 3). Later, when Jesus was asked why he did not show himself to the whole world but only to them, he replied that both he and his father would love all believers, but not those who refuse to obey his teaching.

Paul makes a number of relevant statements, the first being in Romans 6:7 when referring to those who have died to sin. He says that we should no longer be slaves to sin because those who have "died" have been set free from sin. Douglas Moo[8] explains that, whilst believers are not oblivious to the enticements of sin, sin is no longer the master to which they are slaves. In Romans 8:38–39 Paul says that, despite the sufferings that we might have to endure, nothing, including life or death, height or depth, can separate us from the love of Jesus. Paul continues in 10:13 by confirming that everyone who calls on God will be saved, because he is Lord of all and, in 12:2, Paul urges his readers not to conform to worldly patterns but to transform and renew their minds. As Moo states, this means that Christians now belong in a new realm and they should renew their minds and approve what God's will is.

Paul continues with similar sentiments in his letters to the Corinthians. In the first letter 3:16–17 he says that we are God's

7. Keener, *Matthew*, 155.

8. Moo, "Romans," 1115–60.

temple (that is, the sanctuary in which the Spirit dwells)[9] and, if anyone destroys God's temple, God will destroy that person. He repeats this analogy a little further on in verse 6:19, saying that our bodies are the temples of the Holy Spirit, therefore you are not your own. In his second letter to the Corinthians 4:8–9 Paul, who was himself threatened many times during his ministry, says that, although we may be under pressure and persecuted, we are not abandoned or destroyed.

The final reference to Paul on this topic is found in 2 Corinthians 12:7–10 where he earlier refers to a thorn in his flesh, a messenger of Satan, who was sent to torment him. He pleads several times with the Lord to remove it, but was told that God's grace is sufficient for him, and that his power is made perfect in weakness. We are not told the nature of this "thorn", but the underlying message is that one becomes strong through having weaknesses like this. The last of the fourteen citations reflecting the notion that the believer will not perish occurs in Hebrews 13:5–6. Rather than trusting money (that is material things), the writer simply quotes Psalm 118 which states that the Lord is his helper and he will not be afraid, adding: "what can mere mortals do to me?"

It is of interest that these New Testament references on attitudes toward life and death are not too different from those contained in the Old Testament. Once again God does not respond to death wishes and, although we may have to suffer for our faith, we will not be abandoned. We must persevere in the face of challenges, and must remain strong; we must love and not hate. Being anxious achieves nothing. However, unbelievers will not be saved. There is a hint that our lives are predestined, whatever decisions we take.

9. Winter, "1 Corinthians," 1161–87.

CHAPTER 14

SUMMARY AND CONCLUSIONS

THE AIM OF THIS book has been to explore how the Bible can provide guidance on the moral issues of suicide and euthanasia, as well as the more general aspect of coping with despair and life's difficulties. Whereas unassisted suicide is purely the decision of the individual concerned, it was shown that there are different levels of assisted dying, ranging from the most basic "passive" withdrawal of nutrition or life-support, through providing the means for self-administered life termination, to the most "active" administration of a lethal injection by a third party. Whilst there may be less resistance to passive euthanasia in hopeless or persistent vegetative states, some people may wish to draw the line at a more active but still intermediate level.

Others may choose to subsume all premature ending of life measures under the same ethical umbrella, and condemn them as immoral. Conversely, some may accept all forms of premature life termination as acceptable, and the prerogative of the individual concerned, provided this was voluntary. The greatest disagreement concerns active intervention such as providing lethal drugs, even if they are self-administered. Perhaps a genuine concern is that, even if it was legal to do this in the most extreme cases, there is a strong risk of opening the floodgates and broadening the criteria, as now seems to be the case with legalized abortion.

It is therefore not surprising that the whole issue of assisted dying is one that polarizes a large number of people today. As was reviewed in chapter 1, at the present time euthanasia is only permitted in a small number of countries, for example Holland, and Oregon in the USA, and then only under strictly prescribed conditions. Pertinent to this were the actions of American doctor Jack Kevorkian who, in the 1990s before he was jailed for murder when he went a step too far, helped over 130 people to die through the use of prescription drugs (Nicol & Wylie, 2006).[1] In the United Kingdom, a bill permitting assisted dying in carefully defined cases is currently being debated in the British Parliament, but it will have to be reintroduced after the general election in May 2015. On 15th November 2014, the world's media reported that Pope Francis denounced the right-to-die movement, saying that euthanasia is a sin against God. This was a reaction to a recent case in Oregon where a woman took a lethal prescription to end her life, saying that she wanted to die with dignity.

The earlier discussion then addressed the question of the reliability of biblical evidence. Because of the passage of time between the events and their recording in written form, it is not an easy task to tease out the original message, delivered in a different historical and cultural zone to those we have today, and without our current understanding of science and technology. Although what to include in the current biblical canon was very careful considered by eminent scholars over many years, there is still the matter of a lack of original autographs, the many copyings and translations, and no doubt a degree of editing, that has occurred before the modern versions we have today were produced. Readers of a conservative persuasion will nevertheless regard every word in the Bible as accurate and God-given, whereas liberals will adopt a much looser and more subjective interpretation. Added to this is the question of whether the texts should be interpreted literally, or allegorically.

Even assuming we can reach a satisfactory conclusion on the meaning of a text, and the guidance it may offer us on ethical issues, there is still the matter of whether or not we have the free will to follow such guidance. If everything we do is pre-ordained in any event, should we agonize over what is morally right or wrong? If we

---

1. Nicol and Wylie, *Between the Dying and the Dead.*

are worried about being judged in heaven for our deeds on earth, then we have to consider if we shall all be saved regardless of our actions—the universalist view—or whether only those who have already been elected shall be saved—as the particularists maintain. It was previously pointed out that the Bible as a whole contains various types of moral pronouncements, including commands, decrees and examples of virtuous behavior, in addition to the very specific 613 Laws of Moses designed to control just about every aspect of behavior at that time. However, just how many of these apply to us, here and now is a debatable point, apart from those commandments such as not murdering or stealing that have been incorporated into the prohibitions of most if not all countries.

During the review of the fifty-one biblical passages that have been suggested by scholars as being applicable to situations causing despair or contemplated ending of a life, it was evident that very few of them cited an actual or attempted suicide or euthanasia, and in none of these cases was there any obvious moral pronouncement. There were a few death wishes mentioned in both Testaments, but none of these were fulfilled. Based inter alia on selected texts such as these, the main arguments both in for and against euthanasia were then presented, but it would have been rather optimistic to expect a clear winner. Instead, the discussion turned to what the Bible has to say to the believer on more general matters concerning how to cope with life's adversities and despair. What emerged here was a fairly obvious pattern that can be summarized as: keep going and persevere no matter how difficult the situation might be, remain faithful to God and he will look after you. This does not mean we will not suffer, but that we shall not be abandoned. However, most passages indicate that these benefits will not apply to unbelievers.

Whilst this can be used as an argument for never taking one's own life, nor helping someone else to take theirs, none of the situations used in the biblical illustrations are directly related to the modern scenario that the present book is attempting to address. This is the condition of having a painful and terminal illness that leaves the unfortunate sufferer conscious but in a hopeless state, with no chance of recovery, and maybe only being kept alive with the aid of machines. The invalid may decide that he or she is ready to die and, if a believer, in fact looks forward to meeting his or her maker. Is preventing a death in such cases as ethically problematic as ending a life?

If we see a loved one deteriorating into a vegetative state, increasingly unable to have any quality of life and being fully dependent on life-support mechanisms, is it God's will that we take solace from accepting that (only) he gives and takes away (Job: 1:21), or do we feel compelled by compassion to help that loved one end his or her life, if it is clear that he or she requests this? By doing this, would we risk the same fate, even metaphorically, as did the unfortunate Amalekite who was killed by David for complying with Saul's request for euthanasia, assuming that he acted out of compassion (2 Sam, 1:9–10)?

This is certainly not an easy question to answer, but it may help to look at the key arguments from both sides. For those in the "red corner", who oppose assisted dying, the theological arguments usually centre on three sentiments, the first being the commandment not to kill (murder) in Exodus 20:13. The second is that God created human life (Gen 1:27) and has dominion over it: he alone puts to death and brings to life (Deut 32:39), he gives and takes away (Job 1:21), and "there is . . . a time to be born and a time to die" (Eccl 3:2). The third point is that we are to endure suffering: "we glory in our sufferings" (Rom 5:3), "for a little while you may have to suffer grief" (1 Pet 1:6), and "whenever you face trials of many kinds . . . you know that the testing of your faith produces perseverance" (Jam 1:2–3).

In the "green corner", with a more liberal view on assisted dying, the supporting texts include: "love your neighbor as yourself" (Matt 22:37), which Jesus emphasized was one of the two most important commandments; "blessed are the merciful, for they will be shown mercy" (Matt 5:7); and "love each other as I have loved you" (John 15:12). There is also the "golden rule": "do unto others what you would have them do to you" (Matt 7:12), but it has already been pointed out that this is not as applicable to issues such as euthanasia as it might be. If you were an evil person with vices, who welcomes gifts of drugs or alcohol, then plying these on an innocent person would be clearly wrong despite complying with the golden rule. The freedom–determinism debate is also relevant here, with at least some indication that we have freedom over our lives being implied by Paul's statement in Philippians 1:22: "If I am to go on living in the body . . . what shall I choose? I do not know!"

Whilst both camps could claim that they are following biblical guidelines, a difficulty with calling on the Bible to support one's view is that, as already emphasized several times, it is morally neutral on the topic of assisted dying in any form. Thus, citing evidence from the Scriptures runs the gauntlet of proof-texting in an attempt to justify an existing opinion, rather than it being an unbiased enquiry. In a world that is currently more influenced by secular than sacred opinion, it is becoming increasingly difficult to advocate any policy on the basis of Christian ethics alone. The principles of love and mercy exist in the secular world independently of the Bible, so emphasizing that these should be the cornerstones of any decision relating to assisted dying should help to maintain Christian principles, even if they are not specifically acknowledged as such. Thus, what would be the loving and merciful thing to do if a loved one had a terminal illness and pleaded for assistance to hasten death?

Questions such as this are not easy ones to answer but, if faced with them, we can and should pray for guidance. The biblical passages that encourage one to have faith and persevere in the face of adversity offer useful advice, especially in the case of life difficulties other than serious illness. However, some readers will, like the writer, have had close contact with friends and relatives who were very ill and sensed, or were even told, that they knew it was time to let go of life. After a hard life or long illness, it is surely not abnormal if one is to declare that one has had enough, and that it is time to depart rather than try to hang on to the last vestiges of existence in this world. Maybe such a person would welcome a little help to achieve this. The writer hopes that, if faced with such a situation, his wishes would be granted whatever they may be.

CHAPTER 15

THE VIEWS OF OTHER FAITHS

No ENQUIRY WOULD BE complete without comparing the findings gleaned from the Christian Bible with those held by members of some of the other world religions. This final chapter will, therefore, briefly summarize the views that members of the Hindu, Muslim, and Jewish faiths have offered on assisted dying, along with those of the Humanists. Prominent members of each of these groups, plus representatives from the Protestant and Roman Catholic churches, were approached for their responses to four specific questions relating to the premature ending of a life, namely: self-sacrifice, martyrdom, euthanasia, and suicide. The outcomes are given below, and are also summarized in Table 3. A short introduction to each of the non Christian religions is included in the discussion.

CHRISTIAN

The Protestant answers to the four questions were supplied by the Bishop of Peterborough, UK, who emphasized that the views expressed were his own although there was a good deal of agreement within the Church of England on these matters:

Self-sacrifice: is it ethically justified to deliberately take a bullet intended for someone else? The answer was "yes".

Martyrdom: is it ethically justified to accept death rather than relinquish one's faith? The answer was "yes".

Euthanasia: is it ethically justified to actively terminate the life of another at their request? The answer was "no".

Suicide: is it ethically justified to voluntarily and actively end one's own life prematurely? The answer was "no".

The Roman Catholic answers were supplied by the Priest in Charge of St Aidan's RC Church in Northampton, UK. They were identical to those of the Church of England bishop. To underscore the notion that the responses from the two Christian representatives do not necessarily represent the personal view of each and every member of that faith, the UK Daily Mail (28/2/15) reported that the Very Reverend Sandy McDonald said that he would want to end his life if his pulmonary fibrosis condition becomes unbearable. He added that, as far as Christians are concerned, if you love someone you should want them to have a peaceful death.

HINDUISM

The origins of the traditions that ultimately became Hinduism are difficult to date. It is a faith of a cultural unit, originating in the Indus valley in India, but with no single founder.[1] According to at least one source,[2] the words of the holy book Bhagavad-Gita were dictated in 3,137 BC. Geoffrey Parrinder[3] states that the oldest religious books of the Vedas date back to 1,000 BC, but they contain earlier oral traditions that had been passed down for centuries. The Vedas list thirty-three gods of sky, air and earth, of which the god Varuna upholds moral and physical law. Despite these many gods, a form of monotheism exists through the assimilation of many local divinities into Vishnu, who is at one with Śiva. Sri Krishna is the incarnation of Vishnu.

One of the books is the Brahmanas, which comprise commentaries on complex rites, and another is the Upanishads that

---

1. Basham, "Hinduism," 217–54.

2. "Bhagavad-Gita."

3. Parrinder, *Asian Religions*, 31–61.

teach that gods and men are all part of the universal self. The latter also teach of the reincarnation of the soul and its rebirth in a usually endless series of bodies (transmigration), either human or animal, as determined by the "karma" or deeds enacted in the current life. One can only be released through ascetic discipline and moral effort, such that one becomes immortal and a part of the divine being. This is poetically likened to a river entering the sea of which it then becomes a part, losing its personal identity.

The Bhagavad-Gita,[4] written in classical Sanskrit, relates a dialogue between the God incarnate Shri Krishna and Arjuna, who was a warrior leader reluctant to go into battle to reclaim his rightful lands because it would mean killing his kinsman. Krishna reminds him that, in absolute terms, there is no such act as destroying a person. The Atman, or indwelling Godhead, is the only reality and the body is simply an appearance. He tells Arjuna to prefer to die doing his duty. The book neither sanctions nor condemns war, but teaches that a warrior is permitted to kill in battle, as the killing has been determined by God, but it should be done without thought of personal reward. However, the soul is immortal and never dies. The recurring message of the text is to reinforce the morals of kindness, compassion and forgiveness, and the unselfish performance of duty.

Whilst the comments from the Bhagavad-Gita concerning killing in war has some relevance to the end of life topic of this book, other Hindu teaching is more specific.[5] There are two points of view on euthanasia. Whilst on the one hand, helping a person to end a painful life is performing a good deed and fulfilling a moral obligation, on the other hand by helping to take a life, even for compassionate reasons, is disturbing the timing of the cycle of life and death. However, keeping a person artificially alive on a life-support machine also disturbs the natural cycle. Whilst for the same reason suicide is generally prohibited in Hinduism, fasting to death is accepted in the case of spiritually advanced people under specified circumstances, as it is natural and non-violent.

4. *Song of God: Bhagavad-Gita.*
5. "Suicide and euthanasia"

In order to obtain a first-hand view, the writer consulted a Hindu Priest at the Hindu Temple in Wellingborough, Northamptonshire, UK. He was asked the same four questions as were put to the two members of the Christian faith (vide supra). His responses were:

Self-sacrifice: The answer was "no", self-preservation comes first, and God decides when you will die.

Martyrdom: The answer was "yes", it is better to die than to renounce one's faith. Only the body dies; the soul is immortal.

Euthanasia: The answer was "no", that person's life is theirs, not mine to take. Our life has been written.

Suicide: The answer was "no", taking one's own life is a bigger sin than tolerating the hardship of life that you have to endure. God gave you life, so it is wrong to end it prematurely.

ISLAM

Islam is a religion based on the revelations of the prophet Muhammad, who was born in Mecca in about 570 AD and died in 632 AD. He married the widow Khadijah when he was twenty-five years of age, and they had six children. Mecca, and the town of Medina where Muhammad lived for part of his life, are both on a main trade route from Abyssinia to Syria, and he was engaged in the caravan trade (Gibb, 1977).[6] Geoffrey Parrinder[7] explains that Mecca was already a town of pilgrimage before the prophet was born, as visitors came to visit the oblong Kabah building there that was believed to have been built by Abraham, who is acknowledged as ancestor of the Jews, Christians and the Arabs.

When Muhammad was aged forty, the angel Gabriel appeared to him and told him he was the prophet of God, and that he must proclaim the worship of the one God (Allāh) against the

6. Gibb, "Islam," 166–99.

7. Parrinder, *Asian Religions*, 5–20.

prevailing polytheism and idol worship.[8] Gabriel is said to have recited the whole of the Quran, but Muhammad could neither read nor write so he passed the words to others from memory. After his death, the revelations were collected from oral tradition, scraps of written notes and, with perhaps some later additions, were complied into an authoritative text comprising 114 chapters in rhymed Arabic that is the Quran. God is seen as merciful, compassionate and powerful, and is a unity (i.e. not a Trinity). Both Moses and Jesus are recognized as prophets but Muhammad, who denied any suggestion of a supernatural character, is held to be the last and greatest apostle of God.

Muslims have to obey the "Five pillars of faith", which concern prayer, fasting, almsgiving, pilgrimage, and profession of faith. The Quran also contains a great deal of ethical and legal teaching, as well as regulations governing social life such as marriage, divorce and inheritance. Blood revenge is permitted, in that a male next of kin of a slain person has the right to kill the slayer. The death penalty is prescribed for both adultery and apostasy, and a hand can be amputated for theft. H. A. R. Gibb[9] points out that the Quran also teaches that all our actions are predestined, with statements such as "God guides who he wills and turns astray who he wills", although some believe that God has given us the freedom to choose, and that we shall be rewarded or punished according to our works.

This issue of freedom versus determinism is relevant to the assisted dying dilemma, and was discussed earlier in the present book. However, despite capital punishment being permitted in specific cases, Muslims are against both euthanasia and suicide because it is Allāh who decides how long each person will live. According to the Islamic Code of Medical Ethics,[10] it is permitted to discontinue trying to keep alive a patient in a vegetative state, or when death is inevitable, and thus allow the natural process of

8. Gibb, "Islam," 166–99.

9. Ibid.

10. "Euthanasia, assisted dying"

dying to continue. Anything that amounts to failing to resuscitate, or hastening death with pain-killing drugs, is forbidden.

In order to obtain the Muslim response to the same four questions on the ethical justification of assisted dying, a member of the Islamic Association was interviewed. His responses were:

Self-sacrifice: No, it is not ethically justified to take a bullet intended for someone else, as it is God who decides when we shall die. However, it would be acceptable if one fought and even killed the aggressor.

Martyrdom: Yes, one should accept death rather than deny or relinquish one's faith.

Euthanasia: No, God decides when we shall die.

Suicide: No, it is not ethically justified; again it is God's decision when we shall die.

JUDAISM

The history of Judaism is essentially the history of the Old Testament which, as was discussed in chapter 2, began in about 2,000 BC when it is thought that Abraham entered Canaan, with a key event being Moses leading the exodus from Egypt some 500 years later. R. J. Zwi Werblowsky[11] writes that, in ancient times, some "Hebrew" tribes migrated from Mesopotamia to Canaan and then to Egypt. The Patriarchs, who were semi-nomads, appear to have formed cults connected with an anonymous God who had promised Canaan to them. An unknown number of these tribes took part in an exodus from Egypt, probably some time in the mid-thirteenth century BC. These people gradually merged in the major centers to become the nation of Israel, based on the common traditions of ethnic origin, religious beliefs, and cultic practices. Werblowsky suggests that it was during the time of Moses that the concept of "monotheism" developed, based on the acceptance that

11. Werblowsky, "Judaism," 3–39.

the God who adopted Israel as his chosen people was also the creator of heaven and earth, and the sovereign master.

The temple was the centre of the priestly rituals but, when it was first destroyed along with Jerusalem by Nebuchadnezzar in 586 BC, and many citizens were deported to Babylon, this led to the development of community meetings for prayer and instruction. The synagogue came to replace the temple as the centre of worship, and Rabbinic Judaism took over from the priesthood. Its main task was to formulate laws, norms and rules of conduct of which ultimately totalled 613. These governed what one should and should not do, and were often adapted to cover new eventualities. The Hebrew Bible is the same as the Christian Old Testament, but with some rearrangement of the books therein. The first five books (Pentateuch), believed to have been dictated by God to Moses, form the Torah, or Jewish written law.

In the early days there were a number of schools of Judaism, such as the Sadducees who favored Hellenistic culture, the Pharisees who were more conservative and governed by rules, the Essenes with their strong sectarian characteristics, and the Zealots who were political radicals and resisted Roman rule. Currently there are various movements, for example the Karaites, Maimonides, Kabbalists, Messianism, Hasidism, and Reformed Judaism. Maimonides (1135–1204 AD) also spawned a movement, and he is known for formulating "thirteen articles of faith" that comprise the essential dogmas of Jewish religion. These include a belief in the unity of God, the obligation to serve and worship him alone, the resurrection of the dead, and the belief that we are rewarded or punished according to our deeds. A modern development is Zionism, which is a national-cultural organization, in principle a secular movement that stresses the nationhood of Israel rather than a people united solely by the religious bonding. The State of Israel was proclaimed in the year 1948.

With regard to euthanasia and suicide, preservation of life is a supreme moral value of Judaism, and it is forbidden to do anything that might shorten it.[12] Presumably this excludes capital

12. "Euthanasia and suicide"

punishment, which is prescribed several times in the Torah even though it is a last resort, along with killing in legitimate warfare. Even euthanasia to save someone, including the self, from pain does not justify the taking of a life. In keeping with the views of other groups, however, there is no duty to keep someone alive by artificial means if they are in pain or nearing the end of life. Thus, although a doctor can remove an impediment to the natural process of death, both active and passive euthanasia are prohibited.

Responses to the four questions concerning the ethics of the premature ending of a life were supplied by a Rabbi from the Office of the Chief Rabbi, UK, and they included some helpful elaborations. They were:

Self-sacrifice: There is a debate regarding the extent to which a person is allowed to endanger his or her own life in order to save that of another person. Whilst the general consensus is that one can take some risk, but not a significant one, there is a dissenting view that one is permitted to sacrifice one's own life for the sake of another (scored yes?).

Martyrdom: Yes, there is a religious requirement to accept death rather than to relinquish one's faith, as has been demonstrated many times over the course of Jewish history.

Euthanasia: No, this is regarded as a form of murder, although some minor concessions are made regarding certain forms of passive euthanasia.

Suicide: No, this is also regarded as a form of murder, but recent literature has demonstrated sensitivity to the psychological considerations that are often relevant when considering suicide.

HUMANISM

Humanism is not a religious faith, but it is a belief system and is included in this summary for the sake completeness and contrast.

The Dictionary of Human Geography[13] defines Humanism as a secular doctrine that denies that humans are creations of a deity, and it maintains an ethical stance concerned with all that is best about human beings, including civility, generosity, creativity, and empathy. Although there are variations, including religious humanism, humanists generally advocate reason, science and social justice as a basis for ethical decisions, rather than religious dogma and the supernatural. John Cannon[14] explains that humanism is usually associated with the Renaissance in Italy during the fifteenth and sixteenth centuries, with its enthusiasm for rhetoric based on classical literature.

The Humanist Society of Scotland describes the term "secular humanism" as a way of life and thought aimed at bringing out the best in people, and it advocates that we must each take responsibility for our own lives and for the community, whilst rejecting supernatural and authoritarian beliefs. Important tenets are individual freedom, responsibility, tolerance and co-operation. God is excluded from the world, being replaced by human-based approaches to controversial moral issues. Self-determination in matters of life and death is promoted.[15] The Society states that the notions of self-sacrifice and martyrdom have been greatly overvalued in Christian ethics, but that they do not play a major role in a Humanist ethic—in fact the notion of self-sacrifice as symbolized by the crucifixion of Jesus is described as being abhorrent to Humanists.

With regard to assisted suicide and euthanasia, the British Humanist Association (BHA)[16] supports attempts to legalize assisted dying, which includes euthanasia and suicide. Although such actions would be a last resort, their policy is based on the belief that each individual has the right to live according to his or her own personal values, and make decisions about his or her life provided this does not result in harm to others. So long as there are

13. Castree, Kitchen and Rogers, "Humanism."
14. Cannon, *Dictionary of British History.*
15. *Student's Guide to Secular Humanism.*
16. "Assisted Dying"

strict legal safeguards, the BHA states that legalizing euthanasia would eliminate the risk of prosecution faced by compassionate doctors or other individuals who, by one means or another, may be tempted to comply with the pleadings of suffering individuals nearing the end of life to be allowed to die with dignity. It would also remove the necessity of those with the means and ability to travel abroad and have their wishes complied with in countries where euthanasia is legal.

The Humanists do not encourage suicide, but consider it to be a selfish act that ignores the devastating consequences for family and friends left behind. Often, problems that have driven a person to the brink of killing themselves can be resolved if thought through rationally, and therefore less damaging alternative action must be considered.[17] Many causes of suicide can be treated through counseling, medical or psychiatric intervention, and it is considered to be our duty to try and help all who despair through friendship, advice, listening, and providing all the help we can. However, if all this fails to dissuade an individual from the decision to end his or her life, then this should be respected.

Whilst the above information is mostly taken from official policy documents available via the internet, a member of the BHA, who is also licensed to conduct Humanist funerals, provided the following specific answers to the four questions:

Self-sacrifice: It can be right to sacrifice yourself for another, e.g. a parent for a child, but not if your own death will cause more hurt than would be caused by the death of the person you saved, and specifically if that person is a stranger. No, Humanists are not sympathetic to this (scored yes?)

Martyrdom: No, Humanists do not have a faith to relinquish. I would deny being a Humanist if threatened with death, but still continue to uphold the Humanist principles.

17. "Humanist Discussion on Suicide."

Euthanasia: Yes, if it prevents more suffering than it causes, but there must be defined circumstances and appropriate legal safeguards.

Suicide: Yes, it is a rational act if it saves a person from unavoidable, terminal suffering, but again the consequences for loved ones should be considered. If someone who is mentally disturbed seeks to commit suicide, that person should be prevented from doing so because he or she is not acting rationally.

COMMENT

The summary of the views of six different groups, as shown in Table 3, shows that Christians and Jews share the notion that martyrdom is ethically justified, that self-sacrifice can be condoned under specific circumstances, but that both forms of assisted dying are unacceptable. The two Asian religions, Islam and Hinduism, however, whilst also being anti-euthanasia and suicide, are also against self-sacrifice because it violates God's right to decide when a person should die. Martyrdom for one's faith is nevertheless acceptable because this does not deny God. The Humanists accept self-sacrifice under certain circumstances, but not martyrdom. They are also the only group that acknowledges the right of individuals to end their lives through suicide or euthanasia but, again, the circumstances must justify such extreme actions, and must not cause more anguish for others than it saves for the victim.

To refer back to the closing comments of the previous chapter, what would you, the reader, do if faced with any of these four end-of-life situations, either for oneself or a loved one?

Table 3: Ethical justification of four types of premature life endings

	Self-sacrifice	Martyrdom	Euthanasia	Suicide
Protestant	yes	yes	no	no
Roman Catholic	yes	yes	no	no
Hindu	no	yes	no	no
Muslim	no	yes	no	no
Jewish	yes?	yes	no	no
Humanist	yes?	no	yes	yes

BIBLIOGRAPHY

Alexander, T. Desmond. "Exodus." In *New Bible Commentary,* edited by D. A. Carson et al., 92–120. Nottingham, UK: IVP, 2011.

Arnold, Clinton E. "Ephesians, Letter to the." In *Dictionary of Paul and his Letters*, edited by Gerald F. Hawthorne et al., 238–53. Downers Grove: IVP, 1993.

"Assisted Dying," British Humanist Association, March, 2015. https://humanism.org.uk/campaigns/public-ethical-issues/assisted-dying/.

"Assisted dying at Swiss Clinic Rises by 25%." *Daily Mail*, March 14th, 2015.

"Assisted Dying Bill (HL)" (March, 2015). http://www.publications.parliament.uk/pa/bills/lbill/2014-2015/0006/15006.pdf.

Basham, A. L. "Hinduism." In *The Concise Encyclopedia of Living Faiths*, edited by R. C. Zaehner, 217–54. London: Hutchinson, 1971.

Bauckham, Richard. "Universalism: A Historical Survey." *Themelios* 42 (1978) 47–54.

Beougher, Timothy K. "Are All Doomed to be Saved? The Rise of Modern Universalism." *Southern Baptist Journal of Theology* 02(1998) 6–24.

The Bhagavad-Gita: Questions and Answers (March, 2015). http://www.bhagavad-gita.org/Articles/faq.html.

Biddle, Mark E. *Deuteronomy, Smyth and Helwys Bible Commentary.* Macon: Smyth & Helwys, 2003.

Bimson, John J. "1 and 2 Kings." In *New Bible Commentary*, edited by D. A. Carson et al., 334–87. Nottingham, UK: IVP, 2011.

Bray, Gerald. *Biblical Interpretation Past and Present.* Downers Grove: IVP, 1996.

Bruce, F. F. "Paul in Acts and Letters." In *Dictionary of Paul and his Letters*, edited by Gerald F. Hawthorne et al., 679–92. Downers Grove: IVP, 1993.

Bruinsma, Reinder. *Matters of Life and Death.* Nampa: Pacific, 2000.

Butler, Trent C, ed. *Holman Concise Bible Dictionary.* Nashville: Holman Reference, 2011.

"Canada to Allow Doctor-assisted Suicide", US & Canada (March, 2015). http://www.bbc.co.uk/news/world-us-canada-31170569.

BIBLIOGRAPHY

Cannon, John. *A Dictionary of British History*. Oxford: University Press, 2009.

Castree, Noel, Rob Kitchin, and Alisdair Rogers, eds. *A Dictionary of Human Geography*. Oxford: University Press, 2013. http://www.oxfordreference.com/view/10.1093/acref/9780199599868.001.0001/acref-9780199599868.

Chambers Dictionary (2001). Edinburgh: Harrap.

Clines, David J. A. "Job." In *New Bible Commentary*, edited by D. A. Carson et al., 459–84. Nottingham, UK: IVP, 2011.

Cole, Alan. "Mark." In *New Bible Commentary*, edited by D. A. Carson et al., 946–77. Nottingham, UK: IVP, 2011.

Cook, Donald. *The Moral Maze*. London: SPCK, 1992.

Couch, Mal. "Inerrancy: The Book of Revelation." *Conservative Theological Journal* 05 (2001) 206–16.

Craige, Peter C. *The Book of Deuteronomy*. Grand Rapids: Eerdmans, 1976.

DeVries, Dawn. "Schleiermacher, Daniel Ernst." In *Historical Handbook of Major Biblical Interpreters,* edited by Donald K. McKim, 350–55. Downers Grove: IVP, 1998.

"Dignitas, Our Service" (March, 2015). http://www.dignitas.ch.

Dockery, David S. "The History of Pre-critical Biblical Interpretation." *Faith and Mission* 10 (1992) 1–30.

Eaton, Michael A. "Ecclesiastes." In *New Bible Commentary*, edited by D. A. Carson et al., 609–18. Nottingham, UK: IVP, 2011.

Ellingworth, Paul. *The Epistle to the Hebrews*. London: Epworth, 1991.

Erickson, Millard. J. *Christian Theology*. Grand Rapids: Baker, 1985.

———. "Euthanasia and Christian Ethics." *Journal of the Evangelical Theological Society* 19 (1976) 15–24.

Essex, Keith H. "Euthanasia." *Masters Seminary Journal* 11 (2000) 192-215.

"Euthanasia and Suicide," (March, 2015). http://www.bbc.co.uk/religion/religions/judaism/jewishethics/euthanasia.shtml

"Euthanasia, Assisted Dying, Suicide and Medical Ethics." (March, 2015). http://www.bbc.co.uk/religion/religions/islam/islamethics/euthanasia.shtml.

"Euthanasia, Overview" (March 2015). http://www.government.nl/issues/euthanasia.

Evans, Louis H. *The Communicator's Commentary: Hebrews*. Milton Keynes, UK: Word Publishing, 1986.

Fairburn, Donald. "Historical and Theological Studies. Patristic Exegesis and Theology: The Cart and the Horse." *Westminster Theological Journal* 69 (2007) 1–30.

France, Richard T. "Matthew." In *New Bible Commentary*, edited by D. A. Carson et al., 904-45. Nottingham, UK: IVP, 2011.

Fee, Gordon D., and Douglas Stuart. *How to Read the Bible for All its Worth*. Bletchley, UK: Scripture Union, 2001.

Friberg, Timothy, Barbara Friberg, and Neva F. Miller. *Analytical Lexicon of the Greek New Testament*. Crewe, UK: Trafford, 2005.

BIBLIOGRAPHY

Geivett, R. Douglas. "'Misgivings' and 'Openness'. A Dialogue on Inclusiveness Between R. Douglas Geivett and Clark Pinnock." *Southern Baptist Journal of Theology* 02 (1998) 26–37.

Gibb, H. A. R. "Islam." In *The Concise Encyclopedia of Living Faiths*, edited by R. C. Zaehner, 166–99. London: Hutchinson, 1971.

Geisler, Norman L. *Christian Ethics*. Grand Rapids: Baker, 2003.

Gill, Robin. *A Textbook of Christian Ethics* (3rd ed.). London: T & T Clark, 2006.

Grant, R. M., and D. Tracy. *A Short History of the Interpretation of the Bible.* London: SCM Press, 1984.

Guthrie, Donald. *New Testament Introduction*. Downers Grove: IVP, 1970.

Guthrie, George H. "Hebrews." In *Commentary on the New Testament Use of the Old Testament*, edited by G. K. Beale and D. A. Carson, 919–95. Grand Rapids: Baker, 2007.

Hamilton, James M. "Still Sola Scriptura: An Evangelical view of Scripture." In *The Sacred Text: Excavating the Texts, Exploring the Interpretations, and Engaging in the Theologies of the Christian Scriptures*, edited by Michael Bird and Michael Pahl, 215–40. Gorglas Précis Portfolios 7. Piscataway: Gorglas, 2010.

Harrison, Roland K. "Jeremiah and Lamentations: An Introduction and Commentary." *Tyndale Old Testament Commentaries, Vol. 21*. Downers Grove: IVP, 1973.

Hawthorne, Gerald F. (1993). "Philippians, Letter to the." In *Dictionary of Paul and his Letters,* edited by Gerald F. Hawthorne et al., 707–13. Leicester, UK: IVP, 1993.

Helm, Paul. "Universalism and the Threat of Hell." *Trinity Journal* 04 (1983) 35–43.

Hock, Evan C. "Theology and Ethics." *Reformation and Revival* 05 (1996) 33–48.

Holewa, Kathryn A. "Palliative Care—The Empowering Alternative: A Roman Catholic Perspective." *Trinity Journal* 24 (2003) 208–21.

Holmes, Arthur F. *Ethics: Approaching Moral Decisions*. Downers Grove: IVP, 1984.

Houlden, J. L. *Ethics and the New Testament*. London: Mowbrays, 1979.

"A Humanist Discussion on Suicide," March, 2015. https://humanism.org.uk/campaigns/public-ethical-issues/assisted-dying/.

Kannengiesser, Charles. "Antiochene and Syrian Traditions." In *Historical Handbook of Major Biblical Interpreters,* edited by Donald K. McKim, 1–16. Downers Grove: IVP, 1998.

Keener, Craig S. *Matthew*. Downers Grove: IVP, 1997.

———. *Revelation: The NIV Application Commentary.* Grand Rapids: Zondervan, 2000.

Klein, Wiliam W., Craig L. Blomberg, and Robert L. Hubbard. *Introduction to Biblical Interpretation*. Dallas: Word Publishing, 1993.

BIBLIOGRAPHY

Küng, Hans. "'Euthanasia' from 'A dignified dying?'". In *A Textbook of Christian Ethics* (3rd ed.), edited by R. Gill, 381-7. London: T & T Clark, 2006.

Lazenby, Chris. "Do Christians Exercise Free Will?" First Year Lecture on Module TH4609, Broadstairs, UK: Kings Evangelical Divinity School, 2012.

Lindsell, Harold. "Universalism Today, Part 1." *Bibliotheca Sacra* 121 (1964) 209-217.

Longenecker, Richard N. *New Testament Social Ethics for Today*. Grand Rapids: Eerdmans, 1984.

Longman, Tremper, and Raymond B. Dillard. *An Introduction to the Old Testament*. Nottingham, UK: IVP, 2007.

Lowis, Michael J. "A Novel Method to Study the Propensity to Appreciate Music." *Creativity Research Journal* 16 (2004) 105-111.

Mackintosh, Robert. "Universalism." In *A Dictionary of Christ and the Gospels*, edited by James Hastings, 783-786. Edinburgh: T & T Clark, 1927.

Marsh, John. *Saint John*. Harmondsworth, UK: Penguin, 1972.

Marshall, I. Howard. *Acts*. Tyndale New Testament Commentaries. Leicester, UK: IVP, 1994.

Mayhue, Richard L. "Hell: Never, Forever, or Just For a While?" *The Master's Seminary Journal* 9 (1998) 129-45.

McCartney, Dan, and Charles Clayton. *Let the Reader Understand: A Guide to Interpreting and Applying the Bible* (2nd ed.). Phillipsburg: P & R Publishing, 2002.

McDonald. Bruce A. "Theodore of Mopsuestia." In *Historical Handbook of Major Biblical Interpreters*, edited by Donald K. McKim, 65-9. Downers Grove: IVP, 1998.

McKnight, Scot. *Interpreting the Synoptic Gospels*. Grand Rapids: Baker, 1988.

Mckenzie, Michael. "Christian Norms in the Ethical Square: An Impossible Dream?" *Journal of the Evangelical Theological Society* 38 (1995) 413-28.

McQuilkin, Robertson. *Understanding and Applying the Bible*. Chicago: Moody, 2009.

Meilaender, Gilbert. "On Removing Food and Water." In *Readings in Christian Ethics*, edited by David K. Clark and Robert V. Rakestraw, 109-15. Grand Rapids: Baker, 1998.

Mitchell, Margaret M. "Chrysostom, John Part 1." In *Historical Handbook of Major Biblical Interpreters*, edited by Donald K. McKim, 28-349. Downers Grove: IVP, 1998.

Moo, Douglas J. *Encountering the Book of Romans*. Grand Rapids: Baker, 2002.

———. "Romans." In *New Bible Commentary*, edited by D. A. Carson et al., 1115-60. Nottingham, UK: IVP, 2011.

Moreland, J. P. "The Morality of Suicide: Issues and Opinions." *Bibliotheca Sacra* 148 (1991) 214-31.

Morris, Leon. "1 John." In *New Bible Commentary*, edited by D. A. Carson et al., 1397-1409. Nottingham, UK: IVP, 2011.

BIBLIOGRAPHY

————. *Luke*. Tyndale New Testament Commentaries. Leicester, UK: IVP, 1999.

Motyer, J. A. "The Psalms." In *New Bible Commentary,* edited by D. A. Carson et al., 485–583. Nottingham, UK: IVP, 2011.

Moule, C. F. D. *The Gospel According to Mark*. Cambridge: University Press, 1978.

Nassif, Bradley. "Origen." In *Historical Handbook of Major Biblical Interpreters,* edited by Donald K. McKim, 52–60. Downers Grove: IVP, 1998.

Neil, W. *The Epistle to the Hebrews: Introduction and Commentary*. London: SCM Press, 1959.

Nicol, Neil, and Harry Wylie. *Between the Dying and the Dead*. London: Vision, 2006.

Norris, R. A. "Antiochene Interpretation." In *A Dictionary of Biblical Interpretation,* edited by R. J. Coggins and J. L. Houlden, 29–32. London: SCM Press, 1990.

Osborne, Grant R. *The Hermeneutical Spiral*. Downers Grove: IVP, 1991.

Parrinder, Geoffrey. *Asian Religions*. London: Sheldon, 1977.

Parsons, Mikeal C. "Son and High Priest: A Study in the Christology of Hebrews." *Evangelical Quarterly* 60 (1988) 195–216.

Payne, David F. *Deuteronomy: The Daily Bible Study*. Edinburgh: The Saint Andrew Press, 1985.

Payne, David F. "1 and 2 Samuel." In *New Bible Commentary,* edited by D. A. Carson et al., 296–333. Nottingham, UK: IVP, 2011.

Peterson, David "Hebrews." In *New Bible Commentary,* edited by D. A. Carson et al., 1321–53. Nottingham, UK: IVP, 2011.

Pettegrew, Larry D. "Theology and the Basis of Ethics." *Masters Seminary Journal* 11 (2000) 139–54.

Polhill, John B. "Antioch's Contribution to Christianity." *Faith and Mission* 18 (2000) 3–19.

Rakestraw, Robert V. "The Persistent Vegetative State and the Withdrawal of Nutrition and Hydration." In *Readings in Christian Ethics*, edited by David K. Clark and Robert V. Rakestraw, 116-131. Grand Rapids: Baker, 1998.

Rhodes, Ella "We Should bring Death Back to Life into the Open". *The Psychologist* 27 (2014) 648–9.

Russell, Walt. "Insights from Postmodernism's Emphasis on Interpretive Communities in the Interpretation of Romans 7." *Journal of the Evangelical Theological Society* 37 (1994) 511–29.

Schreiner, Thomas R. "Editorial: The Importance of Ethics." *Southern Baptist Journal of Theology* 04 (2000) 1–3.

————. *Romans*. Grand Rapids: Baker, 1998.

Schurer, Emil. *The History of the Jewish people in the Age of Jesus Christ*. Edinburgh: T & T Clark, 1973.

The Song of God: Bhagavad-Gita. Translated by Swami Prabhavanda and Christopher Isherwood. London: Phoenix House, 1972.

BIBLIOGRAPHY

Stallard, Mike. "Literal Interpretation: The key to Understanding the Bible." *Journal of Ministry and Theology* 04 (2000) 14–55.

Stewart, Garry P. "Suicide and the Christian Worldview." *Conservative Theological Journal* 01 (1997) 203–19.

Stuart, Douglas. "Jonah." In *New Bible Commentary*, edited by D. A. Carson et al., 814–21. Nottingham, UK: IVP, 2011.

"A Student's Guide to Secular Humanism," (March, 2015). http://humanism-scotland.org.uk/content/resources/A-Students-Guide-to-Secular-Humanism.pdf.

"Suicide and Euthanasia in Hinduism – ReligionFacts," (March, 2015). http://religionfacts.com/euthanasia/hinduism.htm.

"Suicides in the United Kingdom 2012 Registrations," Key Points (March 2015). http://www.ons.gov.uk/ons/dcp171778_351100.pdf.

Turner, Max. "Ephesians." In *New Bible Commentary*, edited by D. A. Carson et al., 1222–44. Nottingham, UK: IVP, 2011.

Van den Brink, Gils. *Commentary on the Gospel of Matthew.* Elim Evangelical Community, 1977. http://www.elim.nl/theologymatthew.html.

Wallace, Daniel B. *Hebrews: Introduction, Argument, and Outline.* Dallas Theological Seminary, Biblical Studies Press, 2000.

"We Should Bring Death Back to Life, into the Open." *Bibliotheca Sacra* 27 (1914) 648–9.

Webb, Barry G. "Judges." In *New Bible Commentary*, edited by D. A. Carson et al., 261–86. Nottingham, UK: IVP, 2011.

Werblowsky, R. J. Zwi. "Judaism, or the Religion of Israel." In *The Concise Encyclopedia of Living Faiths*, edited by R. C. Zaehner, 3–39. London: Hutchinson, 1971.

Wheaton, David H. "1 Peter." In *New Bible Commentary*, edited by D. A. Carson et al., 1369–85. Nottingham, UK: IVP, 2011.

Winter, Bruce. "1 Corinthians." In *New Bible Commentary*, edited by D. A. Carson et al., 1161–87. Nottingham, UK: IVP, 2011.

Woods, Andy M. "The Purpose of Matthew's Gospel – Part 1." *Journal of Dispensational Theology* 11 (2007) 5–19.

Wright, Christopher J. H. "The Ethical Authority of the Old Testament: A Survey of Approaches. Part 1." *Tyndale Bulletin* 43 (1992) 101–120.

Wylie, Amanda B. "Clement of Alexandria." In *Historical Handbook of Major Biblical Interpreters*, edited by Donald K. McKim, 35–39. Downers Grove: IVP, 1998.

Young, Frances. "Alexandrian Interpretation." In *A Dictionary of Biblical Interpretation*, edited by R. J. Coggins and J. L. Houlden, 10–12. London: SCM Press, 1990.